D1536531

# THE ENVIRONMENTAL FOOD CRISIS

## THE ENVIRONMENT'S ROLE IN AVERTING FUTURE FOOD CRISES

A UNEP RAPID RESPONSE ASSESSMENT

Christian Nellemann *(Editor in chief)*
Monika MacDevette
Ton Manders
Bas Eickhout
Birger Svihus
Anne Gerdien Prins
Bjørn P. Kaltenborn

# PREFACE

In 2008 food prices surged plunging millions back into hunger and triggering riots from Egypt to Haiti and Cameroon to Bangladesh. Whereas fuel prices, which also surged, have fallen back sharply food prices remain problematic with wheat, corn and soya still higher than they were 12-18 months ago.

In order to understand the factors underpinning the food crisis and to assess trends, UNEP commissioned a Rapid Response team of internal and international experts. Their conclusions are presented in this report launched during UNEP's 25th Governing Council/Global Ministerial Environment Forum.

Several factors have been at work including speculation in commodity markets, droughts and low stocks. The contribution of growing non-food crops such as biofuels is also discussed. Importantly the report also looks to the future. Was 2008 an aberration or a year foreshadowing major new trends in food prices and if so, how should the international community respond?

The experts argue that, unless more sustainable and intelligent management of production and consumption are undertaken food prices could indeed become more volatile and expensive in a world of six billion rising to over nine billion by 2050 as a result of escalating environmental degradation. Up to 25% of the world food production may become 'lost' during this century as a result of climate change, water scarcity, invasive pests and land degradation.

Simply cranking up the fertilizer and pesticide-led production methods of the 20th Century is unlikely to address the challenge. It will increasingly undermine the critical natural inputs and nature-based services for agriculture such as healthy and productive soils; the water and nutrient recycling of forests to pollinators such as bees and bats.

The report makes seven significant recommendations. These include real opportunities for boosting aquaculture and fish farming without intensifying damage to the marine environment alongside ones highlighting the opportunities for minimizing and utilizing food wastes along the supply chain right up to consumers.

In response to the food, fuel and financial crises of 2008 UNEP launched its Global Green New Deal and Green Economy initiatives: food is very much part of the imperative for transformational economic, social and environmental change. We need a green revolution but one with a capital G if we are to balance the need for food with the need to manage the ecosystems that underpin sustainable agriculture in the first place.

This report will make an important contribution to the debate but equally it needs to trigger more rational, creative, innovative and courageous action and investment to steer 21st Century agriculture onto a sustainable Green Economy path.

**Achim Steiner**
UN Under-Secretary General and Executive Director, UNEP

# SUMMARY

The surge in food prices in the last years, following a century of decline, has been the most marked of the past century in its magnitude, duration and the number of commodity groups whose prices have increased. The ensuing crisis has resulted in a 50–200% increase in selected commodity prices, driven 110 million people into poverty and added 44 million more to the undernourished. Elevated food prices have had dramatic impacts on the lives and livelihoods, including increased infant and child mortality, of those already undernourished or living in poverty and spending 70–80% of their daily income on food. Key causes of the current food crisis are the combined effects of speculation in food stocks, extreme weather events, low cereal stocks, growth in biofuels competing for cropland and high oil prices. Although prices have fallen sharply since the peak in July 2008, they are still high above those in 2004 for many key commodities. The underlying supply and demand tensions are little changed from those that existed just a few months ago when these prices were close to all-time highs.

The demand for food will continue to increase towards 2050 as a result of population growth by an additional 2.7 billion people, increased incomes and growing consumption of meat. World food production also rose substantially in the past century, primarily as a result of increasing yields due to irrigation and fertilizer use as well as agricultural expansion into new lands, with little consideration of food energy efficiency. In the past decade, however, yields have nearly stabilized for cereals and declined for fisheries. Aquaculture production to just maintain the current dietary proportion of fish by 2050 will require a 56% increase as well as new alternatives to wild fisheries for the supply of aquaculture feed.

Lack of investments in agricultural development has played a crucial role in this levelling of yield increase. It is uncertain whether yield increases can be achieved to keep pace with the growing food demand. Furthermore, current projections of a required 50% increase in food production by 2050 to sustain demand have not taken into account the losses in yield and land area as a result of environmental degradation.

The natural environment comprises the entire basis for food production through water, nutrients, soils, climate, weather and insects for pollination and controlling infestations. Land degradation, urban expansion and conversion of crops and cropland for non-food production, such as biofuels, may reduce the required cropland by 8–20% by 2050, if not compensated for in other ways. In addition, climate change will increasingly take effect by 2050 and may cause large portions of the Himalayan glaciers to melt, disturb monsoon patterns, and result in increased floods and seasonal drought on irrigated croplands in Asia, which accounts for

25% of the world cereal production. The combined effects of climate change, land degradation, cropland losses, water scarcity and species infestations may cause projected yields to be 5–25% short of demand by 2050. Increased oil prices may raise the cost of fertilizer and lower yields further. If losses in cropland area and yields are only partially compensated for, food production could potentially become up to 25% short of demand by 2050. This would require new ways to increase food supply.

Consequently, two main responses could occur. One is an increased price effect that will lead to additional under- and malnourishment in the world, but also higher investments in agricultural development to offset (partly) decreases in yield. The other response may be further agricultural expansion at the cost of new land and biodiversity. Conventional compensation by simple expansion of croplands into low-productive rain-fed lands would result in accelerated loss of forests, steppe or other natural ecosystems, with subsequent costs to biodiversity and further loss of ecosystem services and accelerated climate change. Over 80% of all endangered birds and mammals are threatened by unsustainable land use and agricultural expansion. Agricultural intensification in Europe is a major cause of a near 50% decline in farmland birds in this region in the past three decades.

Taking into account these effects, world price of food is estimated to become 30–50% higher in coming decades and have greater volatility. It is uncertain to what extent farmers in developing countries will respond to price effects, changes in yield and available cropland area. Large numbers of the world's small-scale farmers, particularly in central Asia and Africa, are constrained by access to markets and the high price of inputs such as fertilizers and seed. With lack of infrastructure, investments, reliable institutions (e.g., for water provision) and low availability of micro-finance, it will become difficult to increase crop production in those regions where it is needed the most. Moreover,

trade and urbanization affect consumer preferences in developing countries. The rapid diversification of the urban diet cannot be met by the traditional food supply chain in the hinterland of many developing countries. Consequently, importing food to satisfy the changing food demand could be easier and less costly than acquiring the same food from domestic sources.

Higher regional differentiation in production and demand will lead to greater reliance on imports for many countries. At the same time, climate change could increase the variability in annual production, leading also to greater future price volatility and subsequent risk of speculation. Without policy intervention, the combined effects of a short-fall in production, greater price volatility and high vulnerability to climate change, particularly in Africa, could result in a substantial increase in the number of people suffering from under-nutrition – up from the current 963 million.

However, rather than focussing solely on increasing production, food security can be increased by enhancing supply through optimizing food energy efficiency. Food energy efficiency is our ability to minimize the loss of energy in food from harvest potential through processing to actual consumption and recycling. By optimizing this chain, food supply can increase with much less damage to the environment, similar to improvements in efficiency in the traditional energy sector. Firstly, developing alternatives to the use of cereal in animal feed, such as by recycling waste and using fish discards, could sustain the energy demand for the entire projected population growth of over 3 billion people and a 50% increase in aquaculture. Secondly, reducing climate change would slow down its impacts, particularly on the water resources of the Himalayas, beyond 2050. Furthermore, a major shift to more eco-based production and reversing land degradation would help limit the spread of invasive species, conserve biodiversity and ecosystem services and protect the food production platform of the planet.

# SEVEN OPTIONS FOR IMPROVING FOOD SECURITY

Increasing food energy efficiency provides a critical path for significant growth in food supply without compromising environmental sustainability. Seven options are proposed for the short-, mid- and long-term.

## OPTIONS WITH SHORT-TERM EFFECTS

**1.** To decrease the risk of highly volatile prices, price regulation on commodities and larger cereal stocks should be created to buffer the tight markets of food commodities and the subsequent risks of speculation in markets. This includes re-organizing the food market infrastructure and institutions to regulate food prices and provide food safety nets aimed at alleviating the impacts of rising food prices and food shortage, including both direct and indirect transfers, such as a global fund to support micro-finance to boost small-scale farmer productivity.

**2.** Encourage removal of subsidies and blending ratios of first generation biofuels, which would promote a shift to higher generation biofuels based on waste (if this does not compete with animal feed), thereby avoiding the capture of cropland by biofuels. This includes removal of subsidies on agricultural commodities and inputs that are exacerbating the developing food crisis, and investing in shifting to sustainable food systems and food energy efficiency.

## OPTIONS WITH MID-TERM EFFECTS

**3.** Reduce the use of cereals and food fish in animal feed and develop alternatives to animal and fish feed. This can be done in a "green" economy by increasing food energy efficiency using fish discards, capture and recycling of post-harvest losses and waste and development of new technology, thereby increasing food energy efficiency by 30–50% at current production levels. It also involves re-allocating fish currently used for aquaculture feed directly to human consumption, where feasible.

**4.** Support farmers in developing diversified and resilient eco-agriculture systems that provide critical ecosystem services (water supply and regulation, habitat for wild plants and animals, genetic diversity, pollination, pest control, climate regulation), as well as adequate food to meet local and consumer needs. This includes managing extreme rainfall and using inter-cropping to minimize dependency on external inputs like artificial fertilizers, pesticides and blue irrigation water and the development, implementation and support of green technology also for small-scale farmers.

**5.** Increased trade and improved market access can be achieved by improving infrastructure and reducing trade barriers. However, this does not imply a completely free market approach, as price regulation and government subsidies are crucial safety nets and investments in production. Increased market access must also incorporate a reduction of armed conflict and corruption, which has a major impact on trade and food security.

## OPTIONS WITH LONG-TERM EFFECTS

**6.** Limit global warming, including the promotion of climate-friendly agricultural production systems and land-use policies at a scale to help mitigate climate change.

**7.** Raise awareness of the pressures of increasing population growth and consumption patterns on sustainable ecosystem functioning.

# CONTENTS

# CURRENT WORLD FOOD CRISIS

The current world food crisis is the result of the combined effects of competition for crop-land from the growth in biofuels, low cereal stocks, high oil prices, speculation in food markets and extreme weather events. The crisis has resulted in a several-fold increase in several central commodity prices, driven 110 million people into poverty and added 44 million more to the already undernourished. Information on the role and constraints of the environment in increasing future food production is urgently needed. While food prices are again declining, they still widely remain above 2004 levels.

The objective of this report is to provide an estimate of the potential constraints of environmental degradation on future world food production and subsequent effects on food prices and food security. It also identifies policy options to increase food security and sustainability in long-term food production.

**Figure 1: Changes in the prices of major commodities from 1900 to 2008** reveal a general decline in food prices, but with several peaks in the past century, the last and most recent one the most extreme. (Source: World Bank, 2009).

While food prices generally declined in the past decades, for some commodities, they have increased several fold since 2004, with the major surges in 2006–2008 (Brahmbhatt and Christiaensen, 2008; FAO, 2008; World Bank, 2008). The FAO index of food prices rose by 9% in 2006, 23% in 2007 and surged by 54% in 2008 (FAO 2008). Crude oil prices, affecting the use of fertilizer, transportation and price of commodities (Figures 1 and 2), peaked at US$147/barrel in July 2008, declining thereafter to US$43 in December 2008 (World Bank, 2008). In May 2008, prices of key cereals, such as Thai medium grade rice, peaked at US$1,100 /tonne, nearly three-fold those of the previous decade. Although they then declined to US$730/tonne in September (FAO, 2008), they remained near double the level of 2007 (FAO, 2008). Projections are that prices will remain high at least through 2015. The current and continuing food crisis may lead to increased inflation by 5–10% (26–32% in some countries including Vietnam and the Kyrgyz Republic) and reduced GDP by 0.5–1.0% in some developing countries.

Among the diverse primary causes of the rise in food prices are four major ones (Braun, 2007; Brahmbhatt and Christiaensen, 2008; World Bank, 2008): 1) The combination of extreme weather and subsequent decline in yields and cereal stocks; 2) A rapidly increasing share of non-food crops, primarily biofuels; 3) High oil prices, affecting fertilizer use, food production, distribution and transport, and subsequently food prices (Figure 3); and 4) Speculation in the food markets.

Although production has generally increased, the rising prices coincided with extreme weather events in several major cereal producing countries, which resulted in a depletion of cereal stocks. The 2008 world cereal stocks are forecast to fall to their lowest levels in 30 years time, to 18.7% of utilization or only 66 days of food (FAO, 2008).

Public and private investment in agriculture (especially in staple food production) in developing countries has been declining relatively (e.g., external assistance to agriculture dropped from 20% of Official Development Assistance in the early 1980s to 3% by 2007) (IAASTD, 2008; World Bank, 2008). As a result, crop yield growth became stagnant or declined in most developing countries. The rapid increase in prices and declining stocks led several food-exporting countries to im-

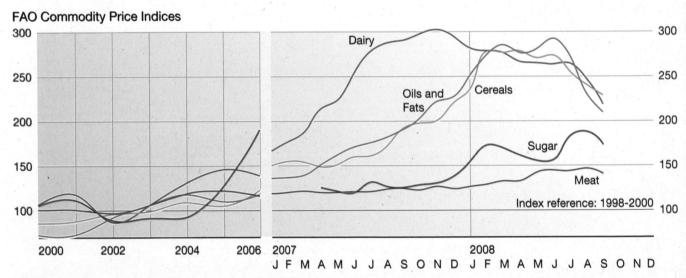

**Figure 2: FAO food commodity price indices 2000-2008.** (Source: FAO, 2008).

pose export restrictions, while some key importers bought cereal to ensure adequate domestic food supply (Brahmbhatt and Christiaensen, 2008). This resulted in a nervous situation on the stock markets, speculation and further price increases.

The impacts of reduced food availability, higher food prices and thus lower access to food by many people have been dramatic. It is estimated that in 2008 at least 110 million people have been driven into poverty and 44 million more became undernourished (World Bank, 2008). Over 120 million more people became impoverished in the past 2–3 years.

The major impact, however, has been on already impoverished people – they became even poorer (Wodon *et al.*, 2008; World Bank, 2008). Rising prices directly threaten the health or even the lives of households spending 50–90% of their income on food. This has dire consequences for survival of young children, health, nutrition and subsequently productivity and ability to attend school. In fact, the current food crisis could lead to an elevation of the mortality rate of infant and children under five years old by as much as 5–25% in several countries (World Bank, 2008). The food situation is critical for people already starving, for children under two years old and pregnant or nursing women (Wodon *et al.*, 2008), and is even worse in many African countries. Although prices have fallen between mid-2008 and early 2009, these impacts will grow if the crisis continues.

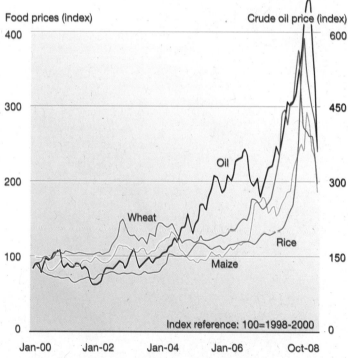

**Figure 3: Changes in commodity prices in relation to oil prices.** (Source: FAO, 2008; IMF, 2008).

# WORLD FOOD DEMAND AND NEED

The growth in food demand and need is the result of the combined effects of world population growth to over 9 billion by 2050, rising incomes and dietary changes towards higher meat intake. Meat production is particularly demanding in terms of energy, cereal and water. Today, nearly half of the world's cereals are being used for animal feed.

## POPULATION GROWTH AND INCOME

Each day 200,000 more people are added to the world food demand. The world's human population has increased near fourfold in the past 100 years (UN population Division, 2007); it is projected to increase from 6.7 billion (2006) to 9.2 billion by 2050, as shown in Figure 4 (UN Population Division, 2007). It took only 12 years for the last billion to be added, a net increase of nearly 230,000 new people each day, who will need housing, food and other natural resources. The largest population increase is projected to occur in Asia, particularly in China, India and Southeast Asia, accounting for about 60% and more of the world's population by 2050 (UN Population Division, 2007). The rate of population growth, however, is still relatively high in Central America, and highest in Central and part of Western Africa. In relative numbers, Africa will experience the most rapid growth, over 70% faster than in Asia (annual growth of 2.4% versus 1.4% in Asia, compared to the global average of 1.3% and only 0.3% in many industrialized countries) (UN Population Division, 2007). In sub-Saharan Africa, the population is projected to increase from about 770 million to nearly 1.7 billion by 2050.

New estimates released by the World Bank in August 2008 show that in the developing world, the number of people living in extreme poverty may be higher than previously thought. With a threshold of extreme poverty set at US$1.25 a day (2005 prices), there were 1.4 billion people living in extreme poverty in 2005. Each year, nearly 10 million die of hunger and hunger-related diseases. While the proportion of underweight children below five years old decreased – from 33% in 1990 to 26% in 2006 – the number of children in developing countries who were underweight still exceeded 140 mil-

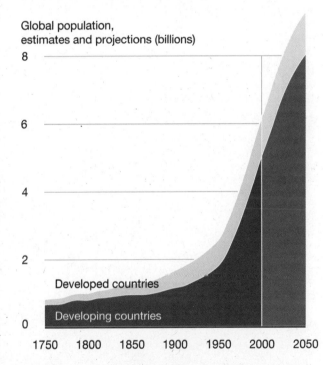

Global population, estimates and projections (billions)

Developed countries

Developing countries

**Figure 4: Human population growth in developed and developing countries** (Mid range projection) (UN Population Division). Continued population growth remains one of the biggest challenges to world food security and environmental sustainability. (Source: UN Population Division, 2007).

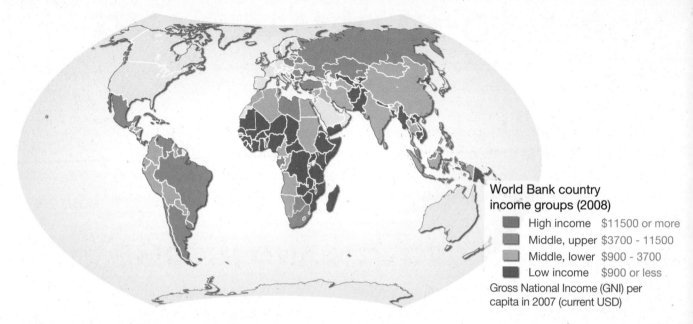

World Bank country
income groups (2008)

| | High income | $11500 or more |
| | Middle, upper | $3700 - 11500 |
| | Middle, lower | $900 - 3700 |
| | Low income | $900 or less |

Gross National Income (GNI) per
capita in 2007 (current USD)

**Figure 5: Incomes are rising, but less so in Africa.** Increased incomes, such as in Asia, generally lead to higher consumption of meat and, hence, increased demand for cereal as livestock feed. (Source: World Bank, 2008).

lion. Similarly, while the proportion of impoverished persons might have declined in many regions, their absolute number has not fallen in some regions as populations continue to rise (UNDP, 2008).

There are huge regional differences in the above trends. Globally, poverty rates have fallen from 52% in 1981 to 42% in 1990 and to 26% in 2005. In Sub-Saharan Africa, however, the poverty rate remained constant at around 50%. This region also comprises the majority of countries making the least progress in reducing child malnutrition. The poverty rate in East Asia fell from nearly 80% in 1980 to under 20% by 2005. East Asia, notably China, was successful in more than halving the proportion of underweight children between 1990 and 2006. In contrast, and despite improvements since 1990, almost 50% of the children are underweight in Southern Asia. This region alone accounts for more than half the world's malnourished children.

In addition to increasing demand for food by a rising population, observed dietary shifts also have implications for world food production. Along with rising population are the increasing incomes of a large fraction of the world's population (Figure 5). The result is increasing consumption of food per capita, as well as changes in diets towards a higher proportion of meat. With growing incomes, consumption – and quantity of waste or discarded food – increases substantially (Henningsson, 2004).

# THE ROLE OF DIET CHANGE

The global production of cereals (including wheat, rice and maize) plays a crucial role in the world food supply, accounting for about 50% of the calorie intake of humans (Figure 6) (FAO, 2003). Any changes in the production of, or in the use of cereals for non-human consumption will have an immediate effect on the calorie intake of a large fraction of the world's population.

As nearly half of the world's cereal production is used to produce animal feed, the dietary proportion of meat has a major influence on global food demand (Keyzer *et al.*, 2005). With meat consumption projected to increase from 37.4 kg/person/year in 2000 to over 52 kg/person/year by 2050 (FAO, 2006), cereal requirements for more intensive meat production may increase substantially to more than 50% of total cereal production (Keyzer *et al.*, 2005).

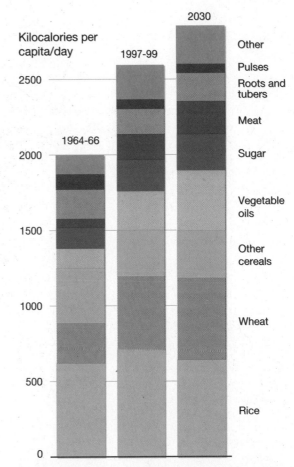

**Figure 6: Changes in historic and projected composition of human diet and the nutritional value.** (Source: FAO, 2008; FAOSTAT, 2009).

# WORLD FOOD SUPPLY

The world food production has increased substantially in the past century, as has calorie intake per capita. However, in spite of a decrease in the proportion of undernourished people, the absolute number has in fact increased during the current food crisis, to over 963 million. By 2050, population growth by an estimated 3 billion more people will increase food demand.

Increased fertilizer application and more water usage through irrigation have been responsible for over 70% of the crop yield increase in the past. Yields, however, have nearly stabilized for cereals, partly as a result of low and declining investments in agriculture. In addition, fisheries landings have declined in the past decade mainly as a result of overfishing and unsustainable fishing methods.

Food supply, however, is not only a function of production, but also of energy efficiency. Food energy efficiency is our ability to minimize the loss of energy in food from harvest potential through processing to actual consumption and recycling. By optimizing this chain, food supply can increase with much less damage to the environment, similar to improvements in efficiency in the traditional energy sector. However, unlike the traditional energy sector, food energy efficiency has received little attention. Only an estimated 43% of the cereal produced is available for human consumption, as a result of harvest and post-harvest distribution losses and use of cereal for animal feed. Furthermore, the 30 million tonnes of fish needed to sustain the growth in aquaculture correspond to the amount of fish discarded at sea today.

A substantial share of the increasing food demand could be met by introducing food energy efficiency, such as recycling of waste. With new technology, waste along the human food supply chain could be used as a substitute for cereal in animal feed. The available cereal from such alternatives and efficiencies could feed all of the additional 3 billion people expected by 2050. At the same time, this would support a growing green economy and greatly reduce pressures on biodiversity and water resources – a truly 'win-win' solution.

# FOOD FROM CROPS

The three primary factors that affected recent increases in world crop production are (FAO, 2003; 2006):

1) Increased cropland and rangeland area (15% contribution in 1961–1999);
2) Increased yield per unit area (78% contribution); and
3) Greater cropping intensity (7% percent contribution).

Trends in crop production and in these three factors are illustrated in Figures 7, 8 and 9.

The use of fertilizers accounts for approximately 50% of the yield increase, and greater irrigation for another substantial part (FAO, 2003). Current FAO projections in food demand suggest that cereal demand will increase by almost 50% towards 2050 (FAO, 2003; 2006). This can either be obtained by increasing yields, continued expansion of cropland by conversion of natural habitats, or by optimizing food or feed energy efficiency from production to consumption.

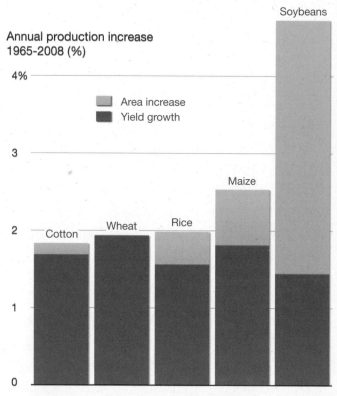

**Figure 7: Production increase in yield and area (1965–2008) of several key crops.** Yield increases have generally exceeded areal increases. (Source: World Bank, 2009).

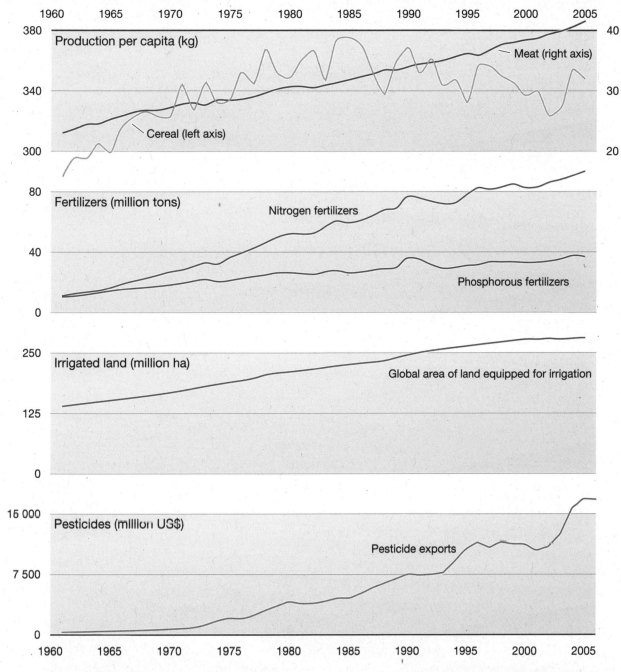

**Figure 8: Global trends (1960–2005) in cereal and meat production, use of fertilizer, irrigation and pesticides.**
(Source: Tilman, 2002; FAO, 2003; International Fertilizer Association, 2008; FAOSTAT, 2009).

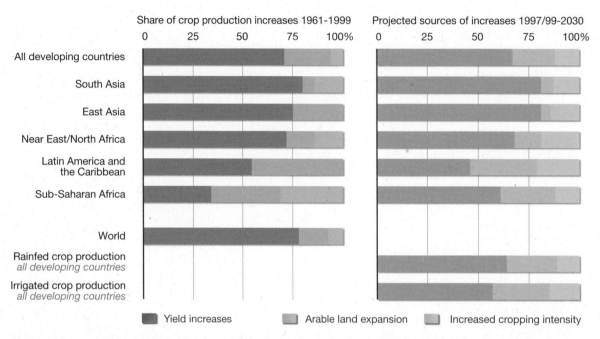

Figure 9: Increase in crop production has mainly been a function of increases in yield due to increased irrigation and fertilizer use. However, this may change in the future towards more reliance on cropland expansion, at the cost of biodiversity. (Source: FAO, 2006).

# FOOD FROM FISHERIES AND AQUACULTURE

Aquaculture, freshwater and marine fisheries supply about 10% of world human calorie intake – but this is likely to decline or at best stabilize in the future, and might have already reached the maximum. At present, marine capture fisheries yield 110–130 million tonnes of seafood annually. Of this, 70 million tonnes are directly consumed by humans, 30 million tonnes are discarded and 30 million tonnes converted to fishmeal.

The world's fisheries have steadily declined since the 1980s, its magnitude masked by the expansion of fishing into deeper and more offshore waters (Figure 10) (UNEP, 2008). Over half of the world's catches are caught in less than 7% of the oceans, in areas characterized by an increasing amount of habitat damage from bottom trawling, pollution and dead zones, invasive species infestations and vulnerability to climate change (UNEP, 2008). Eutrophication from excessive inputs of phosphorous and nitrogen through sewage and agricultural run-off is a major threat to both freshwater and coastal marine fisheries (Anderson et al., 2008; UNEP, 2008). Areas of the coasts that are periodically starved of oxygen, so-called 'dead zones', often coincide with both high agricultural run-off (Anderson et al., 2008) and the primary fishing grounds for commercial and artisanal fisheries. Eutrophication combined with unsustainable fishing leads to the loss or depletion of these food resources, as occurs in the Gulf of Mexico, coastal China, the Pacific Northwest and many parts of the Atlantic, to mention a few.

Current projections for aquaculture suggest that previous growth is unlikely to be sustained in the future as a result of limits to the availability of wild marine fish for aquaculture feed (FAO, 2008). Small pelagic fish make up 37% of the total marine capture fisheries landings. Of this, 90% (or 27% of total landings) are processed into fishmeal and fish oil with the remaining 10% used directly for animal feed (Alder et al., 2008).

In some regions, such as in parts of Africa and Southeast Asia, increase in fisheries and expansion of cropland area have been the primary factors in increasing food supply. Indeed, fisheries are a major source of energy and protein for impoverished coastal populations, in particular in West Africa and Southeast Asia (UNEP, 2008). Here, a decline in fisheries will have a major impact on the livelihoods and wellbeing of hundreds of millions of people (UNEP, 2008).

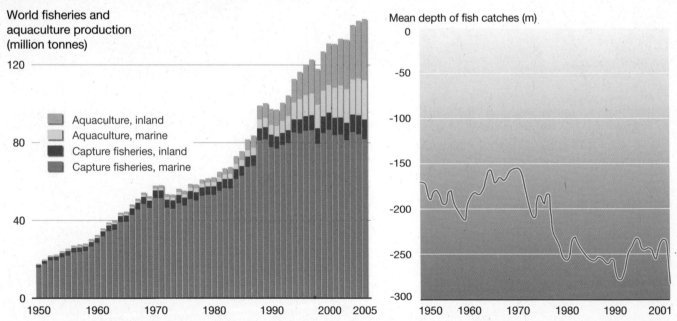

**Figure 10: Fishing has expanded deeper and farther offshore in recent decades** (left panel). **The decline in marine fisheries landings has been partly compensated for by aquaculture** (right panel). (Source: FAO FISHSTAT, MA, 2005; UNEP, 2008).

# FOOD FROM MEAT

Meat production increased from 27 kg meat/capita in 1974/1976 to 36 kg meat/capita in 1997/1999 (FAO, 2003), and now accounts for around 8% of the world calorie intake (FAOSTAT, 2009). In many regions, such as in the rangelands of Africa, in the Andes and the mountains of Central Asia, livestock is a primary factor in food security.

Meat production, however, also has many detrimental effects on the environment, apart from being energy inefficient when animals are fed with food-crops. The area required for production of animal feed is approximately one-third of all arable land. Dietary shifts towards more meat will require a much larger share of cropland for grazing and feed production for the meat industry (FAO, 2006; 2008).

Expansion of land for livestock grazing is a key factor in deforestation, especially in Latin America: some 70% of previously forested land in the Amazon is used as pasture, with feed crops covering a large part of the remainder (FAO, 2006b). About 70% of all grazing land in dry areas is considered degraded, mostly because of overgrazing, compaction and erosion attributable to livestock (FAO, 2006b). Further, the livestock sector has an often unrecognized role in global warming – it is estimated to be responsible for 18% of greenhouse gas emissions, a bigger share than that of transport (FAO, 2006b).

# FOOD FROM ANIMAL FEED

It takes, on average, 3 kg of grain to produce 1 kg of meat, given that part of the production is based on other sources of feed, rangeland and organic waste (FAO, 2006). Currently, 33 % of the cropland area is thus used for livestock (FAO, 2006 livestocks long shadow). In addition, about 16,000 litres of virtual water are needed to produce 1 kg of meat (Chapagain and Hoekstra, 2008). Hence, an increased demand for meat results in an accelerated demand for water, crop and rangeland area. Meat production is energy inefficient and environmentally harmful at industrial scales and with intense use of feed crops such as maize and soybeans. Chicken production is among the most energy-efficient, although still more energy-demanding than cereal production. Many farmers feed their animals organic waste from farm households or agricultural by-products that are unsuitable for human consumption. Small-scale pig farms often use organic residuals from restaurants and the food industry as fodder. If animals are part of an integrated farm production system, the overall energy efficiency can be actually increased through better utilization of organic waste (CTech, 2008). This is not the case for mass production of pigs and poultry in specialized stables, which may take up an increasingly larger proportion of the production of feed crops (Keyzer *et al.*, 2005).

It is also important to note that much meat production takes place on extensive grasslands. But while often a threat to bio-diversity and a source of competition with wild ungulates and birdlife (UNEP, 2001; FAO, 2008b), this requires very little or no input of commercial feed. Furthermore, it plays a crucial role in food security in many mountain areas, as well as in dry and steppe regions, including in Africa, Central Asia and the Andes.

Stabilizing the current meat production per capita by reducing meat consumption in the industrialized world and restraining it worldwide to 2000 level of 37,4 kg/capita in 2050 would free estimated 400 million tons of cereal per year for human consumption – or enough to cover the annual calorie need for 1.2 billion people in 2050. However, changing consumption patterns may be very difficult in the short-term. Increasing food supply by developing alternatives to cereals and improving feed efficiency in commercial feed may however have a much greater potential for increasing food supply (See box).

## FINDING ALTERNATIVE FEED SOURCES

Choice of food – where choice exists – is a complex mix of traditions, religion, culture, availability and not the least, financial constraints. However, while many of these also apply to livestock, our ability to change the feed destined for livestock and aquaculture is probably greater than that of changing people's food choice habits, which are not as easily controlled. As cereal products are increasingly used as feed for livestock, estimated to be at least 35–40% of all cereal produced in 2008 and projected to reach nearly 45–50% by 2050 if meat consumption increases (adapted from FAO, 2003; 2006), finding alternative feed sources provides a huge potential for increasing the

## How many people can be fed with the cereals allocated to animal feed?

By 2050, 1,573 million tonnes of cereals will be used annually for non-food (FAO, 2006a), of which at least 1.45 million tonnes can be estimated to be used as animal feed. Each tonne of cereal can be modestly estimated to contain 3 million kcal. This means that the yearly use of cereals for non-food use represents 4,350 billion kcal. If we assume that the daily calorie need is 3,000 kcal, this will translate into about 1 million kcal/year needed per person.

From a calorie perspective, the non-food use of cereals is thus enough to cover the calorie need for about 4.35 billion people. It would be more correct to adjust for the energy value of the animal products. If we assume that all non-food use is for food-producing animals, and we assume that 3 kg of cereals are used per kilogram animal product (FAO, 2006b) and each kilogram of animal product contains half the calories as in one kg cereals (roughly 1,500 kcal per kg meat), this means that each kilogram of cereals used for feed will give 500 kcal for human consumption. One tonne cereals used for feed will give 0.5 million kcal, and the total calorie production from feed grains will thus be 787 billion kcal. Subtracting this from the 4,350 billion calorie value of feed cereals gives 3,563 billion calories.

Thus, taking the energy value of the meat produced into consideration, the loss of calories by feeding the cereals to animals instead of using the cereals directly as human food represents the annual calorie need for more than 3.5 billion people.

availability of cereal for human consumption. For other feed sources to become a sustainable alternative to the current use of cereals, their exploitation must not be resource-demanding. This poses a big challenge, since most of the easily available feed sources have already been fully exploited, although some alternatives still exist.

Cellulose is the most abundant biological material in the world, but the energy it contains is not readily available for animal production. Due to the interest in using this material for bioethanol production, there are currently large research programs underway to chemically and enzymatically degrade this cellulose into glucose. If this becomes possible and in a cost-

effective manner, wood glucose can, to a large extent, replace cereals as a feed source for both ruminants and monogastric animals. Other fibrous plant sources such as straw, leaves and nutshells are also available in large quantities. Finding ways to feed the world's livestock is therefore a primary challenge (Keyzer et al., 2005).

Other sources for feed that are not fully exploited include seaweed, algae and other under-utilized marine organisms such as krill. However, their potential is uncertain, since technological challenges still remain. In addition, the impact of their harvesting on the ecosystem is of concern. The use of waste provides a much greater potential for alternative sources of animal feed.

# FOOD – OR FEED – FROM WASTE

By using discards, waste and other post-harvest losses, the supply of animal and fish feed can be increased and be sustained without expanding current production, simply by increasing energy efficiency and conservation in the food supply chain.

There has been surprisingly little focus on salvaging food already harvested or produced. An important question centers around the percentage of food discarded or lost during harvesting, processing, transport and distribution as well as at the point of final sale to consumers. Reducing such losses is likely to be among the most sustainable alternatives for increasing food availability.

Discarded fish from marine fisheries is the single largest proportion lost of any food source produced or harvested from the wild. The proportion is particularly high for shrimp bottom trawl fisheries. Mortality among discarded fish is not adequately known, but has, for some species, been estimated to be as high as 70–80%, perhaps higher (Bettoli and Scholten, 2006; Broadhurst *et al.*, 2006). Discarded fish alone amounts to as much as 30 million tonnes, compared to total landings of 100–130 tonnes/year. Feed for aquaculture is a major bottleneck, as there are limitations to the available oil and fish for aquaculture feed (FAO, 2008). A collapse in marine ecosystems would therefore have a direct impact on the prices of aquaculture

## Increasing food supply by reducing food waste

It may be prudent to investigate production and distribution processes and consumption patterns to determine food energy efficiency and the potential food supply, and not merely uncritically increase food production. The efforts to produce food of the highest quality for sale in many countries are often lost simply because the food is thrown away. This reaches up to 30–40% of the food that is produced, processed, transported, sold and taken home by consumers in the UK and USA (Vidal, 2005). Meeting the future global demand for food needs to include enhancing efficiencies of existing production areas and processes, converting wasted food to animal feed and restoring the ecosystems that underpin our ability to feed ourselves.

Food waste is also water waste, as large quantities of water are used to produce the lost food. Undoubtedly, agricultural and food production losses are particularly high between field and market in developing countries, and wastage (i.e., excess caloric intake and obesity) is highest in the more industrialized nations. The loss of, or reduction in other primary ecosystem services (e.g., soil structure and fertility; biodiversity, particularly pollinator species; and genetic diversity for future agriculture improvements) and the production of greenhouse gases (notably methane) by decomposition of the discarded food, are just as important to long-term agricultural sustainability the world over.

Wasting food is not only an inefficient use of ecosystem services and of the fossil fuel-based resources that go into producing them, but also a significant contributor to global warming once in landfills. In the USA, organic waste is the second highest component of landfills, which are the largest source of methane emissions. In the UK, animal digestive processes and manures release close to 40% its methane emissions (Bloom, 2007). Agriculture's contribution to climate change must therefore be considered in the call to increase global food production.

When taken together, post-harvest losses and the wastage of food by both the food industry and consumers call for a concerted effort in raising awareness of the costs to the environment of the inefficient use of nature's resources. Changing the perception of waste as something that needs to be disposed of, to one of waste as a commodity with economic and renewable energy value in the agricultural and food production industries, should be encouraged. Governments can provide support and an enabling policy environment in terms of awareness raising, technology innovation and transfer, agricultural extension to farmers, and support policies that foster managing and recycling of agricultural and food production waste into animal feed. They could also promote policies that take account of the value of ecosystem services, to ensure that ecological needs are also provided for, such as sufficient water in an aquatic nature reserve needed to maintain its proper functioning.

products and on its scale of production. There is no indication that marine fisheries today can sustain the 23% increase in landings required for the 56% growth in aquaculture production required to maintain per capita fish consumption at current levels to 2050. However, if sustainable, the amount of fish currently discarded at sea could alone sustain more than a 50% increase in aquaculture production. However, many of these species could also be used directly for human consumption.

Fish post-harvest losses are generally high at the small-scale level. Recent work in Africa by FAO has shown that regardless of the type of fisheries (single or multi-species), physical post-harvest losses (that is, fish lost for human consumption) are commonly very low, typically around 5% (DieiOuadi, 2007). Downgrading of fish because of spoilage is considerable, however, perhaps as high as 10% and more. Hence, the total amount of fish lost through discards, post-harvest loss and spoilage may be around 40% of landings (DieiOuadi, 2007).

The potential to use unexploited food waste as alternative sources of feed is also considerable for agricultural products. (Figures 11 and 12).

Food losses in the field (between planting and harvesting) could be as high as 20–40% of the potential harvest in developing countries due to pests and pathogens (Kader, 2005). Postharvest losses vary greatly among commodities and production areas and seasons. In the United States, the losses of fresh fruits and vegetables have been estimated to range from 2% to 23%, depending on the commodity, with an overall average of about 12% losses between production and consumption sites (Cap-

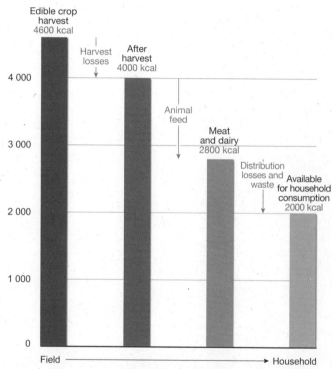

**Figure 12: A gross estimate of the global picture of losses, conversion and wastage at different stages of the food supply chain.** As a global average, in the late 1990s farmers produced the equivalent of 4,600 kcal/capita/day (Smil, 2000), i.e., before conversion of food to feed. After discounting the losses, conversions and wastage at the various stages, roughly 2,800 kcal are available for supply (mixture of animal and vegetal foods) and, at the end of the chain, 2,000 kcal on average – only 43% of the potential edible crop harvest – are available for consumption. (Source: Lundqvist *et al.*, 2008).

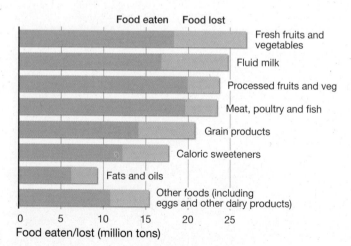

**Figure 11: Food losses for different commodities.** (Source: Kantor *et al.*, 1999).

pellini and Ceponis, 1984; Harvey, 1978; Kader, 2005). Kantor et al (1999) estimated the U.S. total retail, foodservice, and consumer food losses in 1995 to be 23% of fruits and 25% of vegetables. In addition, losses could amount to 25–50% of the total economic value because of reduced quality (Kader, 2005). Others estimate that up to 50% of the vegetables and fruits grown end as waste (Henningsson, 2004). Finally, substantial losses and wastage occur during retail and consumption due to product deterioration as well as to discarding of excess perishable products and unconsumed food. While the estimates therefore vary among sources, it is clear that food waste represents a major potential, especially for use as animal feed, which, in turn, could release the use of cereals in animal feed for human consumption.

In 2007, US$148 billion was invested in the renewable energy market, up 60% from the previous year. Recovering energy from agricultural wastes is becoming increasingly feasible at the industrial production level; investments in technology enhancement of existing systems and innovation in new waste management systems is called for to support this expanding green economy.

## Sustainable food supply

The discourse around food and agriculture that has dominated the past 60 years needs to be fundamentally re-thought over the next few years. New strategies are needed that respond to the daunting challenges posed by climate change mitigation and adaptation, water scarcity, the decline of petroleum-based energy, biodiversity loss, and persistent food insecurity in growing populations. A narrowly-focused 'seed and fertilizer' revolution will not avert recurrent food crises under these conditions; current models of intensive livestock production will be unaffordable; global and national food supply chains will need to be restructured in light of demographic shifts and increasing fuel costs. Future food production systems will not only depend on, *but must contribute positively to*, healthy ecosystems and resilient communities. Soils and vegetation in agricultural landscapes must be restored and managed in ways that not only achieve food security targets far more ambitious than those committed to under the Millennium Development Goals, but also provide watershed services and wildlife habitat, and sequester greenhouse gases.

# Other key facts and figures on food waste and losses

**United States of America:**
In the United States 30% of all food, worth US$48.3 billion (€32.5 billion), is thrown away each year. It is estimated that about half of the water used to produce this food also goes to waste, since agriculture is the largest human use of water. Losses at the farm level are probably about 15–35%, depending on the industry. The retail sector has comparatively high rates of loss of about 26%, while supermarkets, surprisingly, only lose about 1%. Overall, losses amount to around US$90 billion–US$100 billion a year (Jones, 2004 cited in Lundqvist *et al.*, 2008).

**Africa:**
In many African countries, the post-harvest losses of food cereals are estimated at 25% of the total crop harvested. For some crops such as fruits, vegetables and root crops, being less hardy than cereals, post-harvest losses can reach 50% (Voices Newsletter, 2006). In East Africa and the Near East, economic losses in the dairy sector due to spoilage and waste could average as much as US$90 million/year (FAO, 2004). In Kenya, each year around 95 million litres of milk, worth around US$22.4 million, are lost. Cumulative losses in Tanzania amount to about 59.5 million litres of milk each year, over 16% of total dairy production during the dry season and 25% in the wet season. In Uganda, approximately 27% of all milk produced is lost, equivalent to US$23 million/year (FAO, 2004).

**Asia:**
Losses for cereals and oil seeds are lower, about 10–12%, according to the Food Corporation of India. Some 23 million tonnes of food cereals, 12 million tonnes of fruits and 21 million tonnes of vegetables are lost each year, with a total estimated value of 240 billion Rupees. A recent estimate by the Ministry of Food Processing is that agricultural produce worth 580 billion Rupees is wasted in India each year (Rediff News, 2007 cited in Lundqvist *et al.*, 2008).

**Europe:**
United Kingdom households waste an estimated 6.7 million tonnes of food every year, around one third of the 21.7 million tonnes purchased. This means that approximately 32% of all food purchased per year is not eaten. Most of this (5.9 million tonnes or 88%) is currently collected by local authorities. Most of the food waste (4.1 million tonnes or 61%) is avoidable and could have been eaten had it been better managed (WRAP, 2008; Knight and Davis, 2007).

**Australia:**
In a survey of more than 1,600 households in Australia in 2004 on behalf of the Australia Institute, it was concluded that on a country-wide basis, $10.5 billion was spent on items that were never used or thrown away. This amounts to more that $5,000/capita/year.

**Environmental impacts of food waste**
The impact of food waste is not just financial. Environmentally, food waste leads to: wasteful use of chemicals such as fertilizers and pesticides; more fuel used for transportation; and more rotting food, creating more methane – one of the most harmful greenhouse gases that contributes to climate change. Methane is 23 times more potent than $CO_2$ as a greenhouse gas. The vast amount of food going to landfills makes a significant contribution to global warming. WRAP (Waste and Resource Action Program), a UK based group, estimates that if food were not discarded in this way in the UK, the level of greenhouse gas abatement would be equivalent to removing 1 in 5 cars from the road (WRAP, 2007).

# IMPACTS ON ENVIRONMENTAL DEGRADATION ON YIELD AND AREA

The natural environment, with all its ecosystem services, comprises the entire basis for life on the planet. Its value is therefore impossible to quantify or even model. The state of environment has – at any given stage – effects on food production through its role in water, nutrients, soils, climate and weather as well as on insects that are important for pollination and regulating infestations. The state of ecosystems also influences the abundance of pathogens, weeds and pests, all factors with a direct bearing on the quality of available cropland, yields and harvests.

Environmental degradation due to unsustainable human practices and activities now seriously endangers the entire production platform of the planet.

Land degradation and conversion of cropland for non-food production including bio-fuels, cotton and others are major threats that could reduce the available cropland by 8–20% by 2050. Species infestations of pathogens, weeds and insects, combined with water scarcity from overuse and the melting of the Himalayas glaciers, soil erosion and depletion as well as climate change may reduce current yields by at least an additional 5–25% by 2050, in the absence of policy intervention. These factors entail only a portion of the environment covering direct effects. The indirect effects, including socio-economic responses, may be considerably larger.

# THE ROLE OF THE ENVIRONMENT IN FOOD PRODUCTION

There is a strong link between the state of the environment and food production, apart from the natural environment being the entire platform upon which all life is based. For crops, the state of the environment directly influences soil nutrient availability, water (ground and surface water for irrigation), climate and weather (rainfall and growth season), availability of insects for pollination, and not the least, the abundance and effects of cer-tain pests, such as pathogens, insects and weeds, which have ma-jor impact on crops worldwide, particularly in Africa (Sanchez, 2002). Without these services, there would be no production, Ecosystem services enhance agro-ecosystem resilience and sus-tain agricultural productivity. Thus, promoting the healthy func-tioning of ecosystems ensures the sustainability of agriculture as it intensifies to meet the growing demands for food production.

The interaction among these variables is very complex, and providing quantitative estimates of their significance is nearly impossible. The key variables are not currently accounted for in most models and scenarios of food production (FAO, 2003; 2006).

In this chapter we attempt to provide estimates of possible ranges of future impacts of environmental degradation on yield and available cropland, based on the best knowledge available, peer-reviewed studies and expert judgment. We will not, however, attempt to quantify the full value of ecosystem services from the environment, which entail complex interactions and processes.

The estimates given here are of possible ranges based on some current projections of the degree of environmental degradation.

The FAO has provided estimates of cropland and yield increases necessary to meet future demand for food, without fully considering the role of environmental degradation and losses of ecosystem services. Hence, the following material provides an insight into the possible losses (and the compensation needed) in food production as a result of environmental degradation, to support other UN agencies in further improving estimates of demand and production in a changing world.

# LOSS OF CROPLAND AREA

There has been a growing trend all over the world in converting cropland to other uses due to increasing urbanization, industrialization, energy demand and population growth. China, for example, lost more than 14.5 million ha of arable land between 1979 and 1995 (ICIMOD, 2008).

Current projections suggest that an additional 120 million ha – an area twice the size of France or one-third that of India – will be needed to support the traditional growth in food production by 2030, mainly in developing countries (FAO, 2003), without considering the compensation required for certain losses. The demand for irrigated land is projected to increase by 56% in Sub-Saharan Africa (from 4.5 to 7 million ha), and rainfed land by 40% (from 150 to 210 million ha) in order to meet the demand, without considering ecosystem services losses and setbacks in yields and available cropland (FAO, 2003; 2006). Increases in available cropland may be possible in Latin America through the conversion of rainforests (Figure 13), which in turn will accelerate climate change and biodiversity losses, causing feedback loops that may hinder the projected increases in crop yields. The potential for increases is more questionable in large parts of sub-Saharan Africa due to political, socio-economic and environmental constraints. In Asia, nearly 95% of the potential cropland has already been utilized (FAO, 2003; 2006). Even if such increases are not restricted by other land use and the protection of tropical rainforests, changes in the proportion of non-food crops to food crops may have even greater impacts on the available cropland for food production.

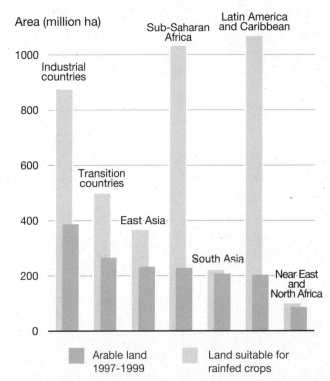

**Figure 13: Theoretical potential for cropland expansion, irrespective of conservation, water and other environmental issues.** (Source: FAO, 2003).

# BIOFUELS AND COTTON – SUSTAINABLE OPTIONS TO INCREASE INCOMES OR THREAT TO BIODIVERSITY AND FOOD PRODUCTION?

Biofuels have grown quickly in demand and production (Figure 14), fuelled by high oil prices and the initial perception of their role in reducing $CO_2$ emissions (FAO, 2008). Biofuels, including biodiesel from palm oil and ethanol from sugarcane, corn and soybean, accounted for about 1% of the total road transport in 2005, and may reach 25% by 2050, with the EU having set targets as high as 10% by 2020 (World Bank, 2007; FAO, 2008). For many countries, such as Indonesia and Malaysia, biofuels are also seen as an opportunity to improve rural livelihoods and boost the economy through exports (Fitzherbert *et al.*, 2008; UNEP, 2008). The US is the largest producer and consumer of bioethanol, followed by Brazil (Figure 15) (World

Bank, 2007; FAO, 2008). Brazil has now used 2.7 million ha of land area for this production (4.5% of the cropland area), mainly sugar cane.

While biofuels are a potential low-carbon energy source, the conversion of rainforests, peatlands, savannas, or grasslands to produce biofuels in the US, Brazil and Southeast Asia may create a "biofuel carbon debt" by releasing 17 to 420 times more $CO_2$ than the annual greenhouse gas reductions that these biofuels would provide by displacing fossil fuels (Fargione *et al.*, 2008; Searchinger *et al.*, 2008). Corn-based ethanol, instead of producing a 20% savings, will nearly double greenhouse emis-

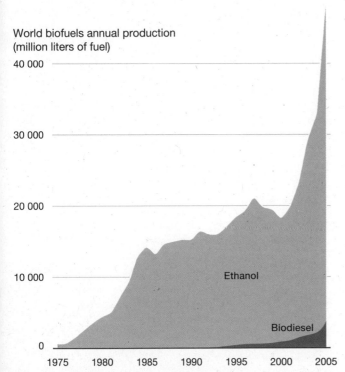

**Figure 14: The production of biodiesel and ethanol has increased substantially in recent years.** (Source: Earth Policy Institute, 2006).

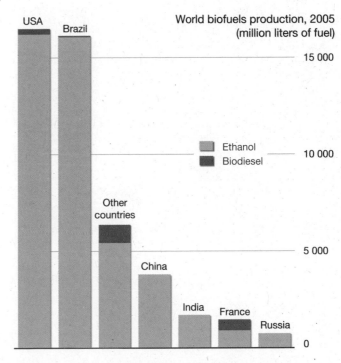

**Figure 15: United States and Brazil are among the greatest producers of biofuels today.** (Source: Earth Policy Institute, 2006).

sions over 30 years (Searchinger *et al.*, 2008). Biofuels from switchgrass, if grown on US corn lands, will increase emissions by 50% (Fargione *et al.*, 2008). It is evident that the main potential of biofuels lies in using waste biomass or biomass grown on degraded and abandoned agricultural lands planted with perennials (World Bank, 2007; FAO, 2008).

Production of crops for biofuels also competes with food production (Banse *et al.*, 2008). Indeed, the corn equivalent of the energy used on a few minutes drive could feed a person for a day, while a full tank of ethanol in a large 4-wheel drive suburban utility vehicle could almost feed one person for a year. A recent OECD-FAO (2007) report expected food prices to rise by between 20% and 50% by 2016 partly as a result of biofuels.

Already, drastically raised food prices have resulted in violent demonstrations and protests around the world in early 2008. Current OECD scenarios by the IMAGE model project a mean increase in the proportion of land allocated to crops for biofuel production equivalent to 0.5% of the cropland area in 2008, 2% by 2030 (range 1–3%) and 5% by 2050 (range 2–8%).

Production of other non-food crops is also projected to increase. For example, cotton is projected to increase to an additional 2% of cropland area by 2030 and 3% by 2050 (Ethridge *et al.*, 2006; FAPRI 2008). Hence, the combined increase in cropland area designated for the production of biofuels and cotton alone could be in the range of 5–13% by 2050 and have the potential to negatively impact food production and biodiversity.

# LOSS OF CROPLAND FROM URBAN DEVELOPMENT

Infrastructure and urban development is increasing rapidly (UN, 2008). Settlement primarily occurred at the cost of cropland, as people historically settled in the most productive locations (e.g., Maizel *et al.* 1998; Goldewijk, 2001, 2005; Klein Goldewijk and Beusen, 2009). Hence, as settlements, towns and cities grow, the adjacent cropland is reduced to accommodate urban infrastructure such as roads and housing. Globally, estimates of the extent of built-up areas in 2000 range from 0.2% – 2.7% of the total land area (Potere and Schneider, 2007)

with 5 of the 7 estimates below 0.5%. Most of the differences can be explained by the various definitions of built-up area and differences between satellite derived and inventory based data. All these percentages relate to about 0.3–3.5 million km² of land worldwide, which at first appear to be unavailable for producing food. However, UNDP (1996) estimated that 15– 20% of the world's food is produced in (peri-)urban areas (although it is not clear whether parts of this peri-urban area are already included in cropland inventories or not; besides there is large uncertainty and variability by city/region of the UNDP estimate).

Preliminary future estimates based on the HYDE methodology (Beusen and Klein Goldewijk, in prep) with the medium population growth variant of the UN (2008) reveal that with an expected increase of the global urban population from 2.9 billion people in 2000 to 5 billion in 2030 and 6.4 billion in 2050, the built-up area is likely to increase from 0.4% of the total global land area in 2000 to about 0.7% by 2030, and to 0.9% by 2050, corresponding roughly to 0.5 million km², 0.9 million km² and 1.2 million km², respectively.

The computed ratio of built-up area/cropland area is 3.5% in 2000, 5.1% in 2030 and 7% in 2050, respectively. This means that if all additional built-up area would be at the expense of cropland (Stehfest *et al.*, 2008), a total of 0.37 million km² of cropland would be lost by 2030, and another 0.30 million km² by 2050.

# LOSS OF CROPLAND AREA FROM LAND DEGRADATION

About 2 billion ha of the world's agricultural land have been degraded because of deforestation and inappropriate agricultural practices (Pinstrup-Andersen and Pandya-Lorch, 1998). In spite of global improvements on some parts of the land, unsustainable land use practices result in net losses of cropland productivity – an average of 0.2%/year. The combined effects of competition for land from growing populations, reduced opportunity for migration and rotation along with higher livestock densities, result in frequent overgrazing and, hence, loss of long-term productivity. Satellite measurements show that between 1981 and 2003, there was an absolute decline in the productive land area (as Net Primary Productivity) across 12% of the global land area. The areas affected are home to about 1–1.5 billion people, some 15–20% of the global population (Bai et al., 2007).

A number of authors including den Biggelaar et al. (2004) estimate that globally, 20,000–50,000 km² of land are lost annually through land degradation, chiefly soil erosion, with losses 2–6 times higher in Africa, Latin America and Asia than in North America and Europe. The major degrading areas are in Africa south of the Equator, Southeast Asia, Southern China, North-Central Australia and the pampas of South America. Some 950,000 km² of land in Sub-Saharan Africa is threatened with irreversible degradation if nutrient depletion continues (Henao and Baanante, 2006). In most parts of Asia, forest is shrinking, agriculture is gradually expanding to marginal lands and land degradation is accelerating through nutrient leaching and soil erosion. In fact, about 20% of the agricultural land in Asia has been degraded over the last several decades (Foley et al., 2005). The pace of degradation is much higher in environmentally fragile areas, such as on the mountains.

# YIELDS

Environmental degradation and loss of ecosystem services will directly affect pests (weeds, insects and pathogens), soil erosion and nutrient depletion, growing conditions through climate and weather, as well as available water for irrigation through impacts on rainfall and ground and surface water. These are factors that individually could account for over 50% in loss of the yield in a given "bad" year. The interactions among these variables, compounded by management systems and society, are highly complex. A changing climate will affect evapo-transpiration, rainfall, river flow, resilience to grazing, insects, pathogens and risk of invasions, to mention a few. In the following section we attempt to provide for each variable, rough estimates of how much environmental degradation and loss of some ecosystem services could contribute to reducing yields by 2050. This is based on peer reviewed studies, models and expert judgment, and with the understanding that conditions and estimates vary considerably and relationships are highly complex.

## IMPACTS OF LAND DEGRADATION ON CROP YIELDS

Unsustainable practices in irrigation and production may lead to increased salinization of soil, nutrient depletion and erosion. An estimated 950 million ha of salt-affected lands occur in arid and semi-arid regions, nearly 33% of the potentially arable land area of the world. Globally, some 20% of irrigated land (450,000 km²) is salt-affected, with 2,500–5,000 km² of lost production every year as a result of salinity (UNEP, 2008).

In South Asia, annual economic loss is estimated at US$1,500 million due to salinization (UNEP, 1994).

Nutrient depletion as a form of land degradation has a severe economic impact at the global scale, especially in Sub-Saharan Africa. Stoorvogel *et al.* (1993) estimated nutrient balances for 38 countries in Sub-Saharan Africa. Annual depletion rates of soil

**Global change in productivity 1981-2003**

| | |
|---|---|
| ■ Decrease | < -20 |
| ■ Slight decrease | -20 – -5 |
| □ Little change | -5 – 5 |
| □ Slight increase | +5 – +20 |
| □ Increase | +20 > |

Change in net primary productivity (NPP) in kg Carbon per hectare, per year

**Figure 16: Losses in land productivity due to land degradation.** (Source: Bai *et al.*, 2008).

## Kenya land use and rain-use efficiency

Sub-Saharan Africa is particularly impacted by land degradation. In Kenya, over the period 1981–2003, despite improvements in woodland and grassland, productivity declined across 40% of cropland – a critical situation in the context of a doubling of the human population over the same period (Bai and Dent, 2006).

In South Africa, production decreased overall; 29% of the country suffered land degradation, including 41% of all cropland (Bai and Dent, 2007a); about 17 million people, or 38% of the South African population, depend on these degrading areas. (Source: Bai and Dent, 2007).

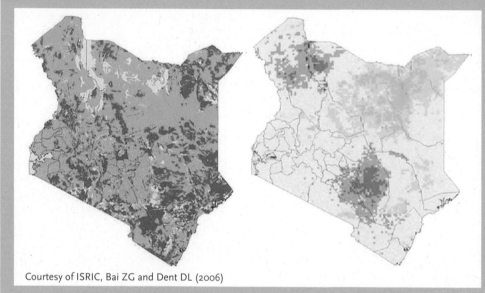

Courtesy of ISRIC, Bai ZG and Dent DL (2006)

**Trend in biomass in 1981–2003 (left) and in rain-use efficiency (RUE) in 1981–2002 (right).** Decreases in RUE could be due to various factors, including degradation and run-off, soil evaporation, increasing depleted soils, overgrazing by livestock or other forms of range degradation.

**Left map**
*Red* urban
*Yellow* cropland
*Green* grassland
*Purple* woodland
*Blue* water

**Right map**
*Red* major decline
*Yellow* moderate decline
*Green* improvement

fertility were estimated at 22 kg nitrogen (N), 3 kg phosphorus (P), and 15 kg potassium (K) per ha. In Zimbabwe, soil erosion alone results in an annual loss of N and P totalling US\$1.5 billion. In South Asia, the annual economic loss is estimated at US\$600 million for nutrient loss by erosion, and US\$1,200 million from soil fertility depletion (Stocking, 1986; UNEP, 1994).

Erosion is very significant in land degradation. On a global scale, the annual loss of 75 billion tonnes of soil costs the world about US\$400 billion/year (at US\$3/tonne of soil for nutrients and US\$2/tonne of soil for water), or approximately US\$70/person/year (Lal, 1998). It is estimated that the total annual cost of erosion from agriculture in the US is about US\$44 billion/year or about US\$247/ha of cropland and pasture (Lal, 1998). In Sub-Saharan Africa it is much larger; in some coun-

tries productivity has declined in over 40% of the cropland area in two decades while population has doubled. Overgrazing of vegetation by livestock and subsequent land degradation is a widespread problem in these regions.

The productivity of some lands has declined by 50% due to soil erosion and desertification (Figure 16). Yield reduction in Africa due to past soil erosion may range from 2–40%, with a mean loss of 8.2% for the continent. Africa is perhaps the continent most severely impacted by land degradation (den Biggelaar *et al.*, 2004; Henao and Baanante, 2006), with the global average being lower, possibly in the range of 1–8%. With increasing pressures of climate change, water scarcity, population growth and increasing livestock densities, these ranges will be probably conservative by 2050.

# IMPACTS OF CLIMATE CHANGE ON YIELD

Global climate change may impact food production across a range of pathways (Figure 17): 1) By changing overall growing conditions (general rainfall distribution, temperature regime and carbon); 2) By inducing more extreme weather such as floods, drought and storms; and 3) By increasing extent, type and frequency of infestations, including that of invasive alien species (dealt with in a separate section).

The estimated impacts of changes in the general climate regime vary with the different models in the short to mid-term (2030–2050), but after 2050 an increasing number of models agree on rising negative impacts (IPCC, 2007; Schmidhuber and Tubiello, 2007). Many models have projected that the potential for global food production may rise with increases in local average temperature over a range of 1–3°C (before 2050),

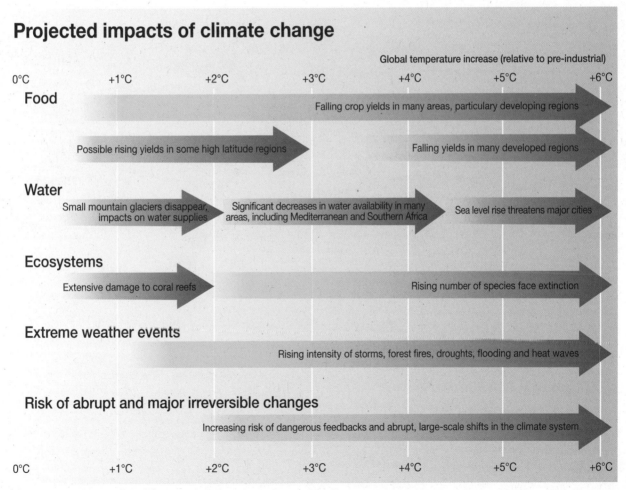

**Figure 17: Projected impacts of climate change.** (Source: Stern Review, 2008).

but above this range (after 2050) may decrease (IPCC, 2007; Meehl *et al.*, 2007). Model projections suggest that although increased temperature and decreased soil moisture will act to reduce global crop yields by 2050, the direct fertilization effect of rising carbon dioxide concentration ($CO_2$) will offset these losses. The $CO_2$ fertilization factors used in models to project future yields were derived from enclosure studies conducted about 20 years ago. Free-air concentration enrichment (FACE) technology has now facilitated large-scale trials of the major grain crops at elevated $CO_2$ levels under full open-air field conditions. In those trials, elevated $CO_2$ enhanced yield by about 50% less than in the enclosure studies. Hence, previous projections of no impact or even a slight positive impact of increasing $CO_2$ on global agricultural production by 2030 and 2050 may be too optimistic (Long *et al.*, 2006). Current research result concludes that while crops would respond posi-

tively to elevated $CO_2$ in the absence of climate change, the associated impacts of high temperatures, altered patterns of precipitation, and possible increased frequency of extreme events such as droughts and floods, will likely combine to depress yields and increase production risks in many world regions (Tubiello and Fischer, 2006).

Furthermore, projected changes in the frequency and severity of extreme climate events are predicted to have more serious consequences for food and food security than changes in projected mean temperatures and precipitation (IPCC, 2007). Also, regional differences will grow stronger with time (Parry *et al.*, 2005), with potentially large negative impacts in developing regions but only small changes in developed regions (IPCC 2007; Slater *et al.* 2007). Developing countries are more vulnerable because of the dominance of agriculture in their econ-

omies, the scarcity of capital for adaptation measures, their warmer baseline climates and heightened exposure to extreme events (Tubiello and Fischer, 2006; Brown and Funk, 2008). This will aggravate inequalities in food production among regions (Parry *et al.*, 2005).

Regional impacts will be strongest across Africa and Western Asia where yields of the dominant regional crops may fall by 15–35% once temperatures rise by 3 or 4° C (Stern Review, 2006). Sub-Saharan Africa is expected to be worst affected, meaning the poorest and most food insecure region is also expected to suffer the largest contraction of agricultural production and income. Despite the uncertainties regarding short-term effects, models do point to many cases where food security is clearly threatened by climate change by 2030, with losses in major crops by this time (Lobell *et al.*, 2008).

There is wide variation in how individual species in different regions respond to a warming climate and Lobell *et al.* (2008) identified 3 general classes of crop responses to climate change projections: 1) Consistently negative, for example, Southern African maize; 2) Large uncertainties ranging from substantially positive to substantially negative, for example, South Asian groundnut; and 3) Relatively unchanged, for example, West African wheat. Adaptation to climate change by switching from highly vulnerable to less vulnerable crops may be viable, and is recommended particularly for South Asia and South Africa where the case for adaptation is particularly robust (Lobell *et al.*, 2008).

The impacts on crops are also highly variable in different regions and on different types of crops. For example, in Southern Africa, declines in production of 15% for wheat and 27% for maize in the absence of any agricultural adaptation to climate change have been projected by Lobell *et al.* (2008). The effects of extreme weather are not included in these estimates. In addition, these effects are projected to 2030 only, when the impacts of climate change would be only just emerging. Increasing our understanding how crops may be impacted under climate change conditions may provide alternatives for adaptive strategies in the most vulnerable regions of the world (Lobell *et al.*, 2008).

Based on a consensus estimate of 6 climate models and two crop modelling methods, Cline (2007) concluded that by 2080, assuming a 4.4° C increase in temperature and a 2.9% increase in precipitation, global agricultural output potential is likely to decrease by about 6%, or 16% without carbon fertilization. Cline suggested a range of output potential decline between 10 and 25% among regions. As climate change increases, projections have been made that by 2080 agricultural output potential may be reduced by up to 60% for several African countries, on average 16–27%, dependent upon the effect of carbon fertilization (Figures 18 and 19). These effects are in addition to general water scarcity as a result of melting glaciers, change in rainfall patterns, or overuse.

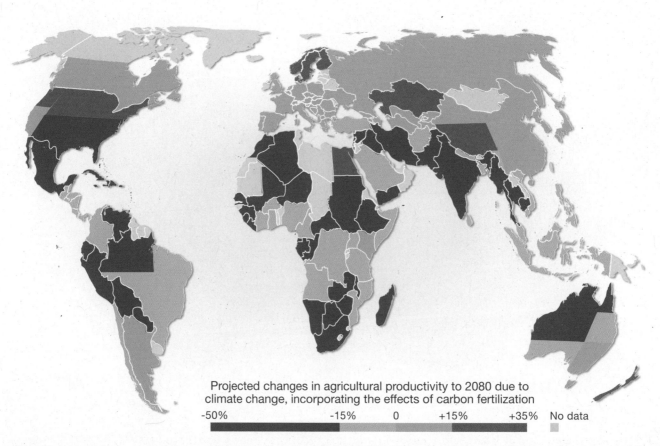

Projected changes in agricultural productivity to 2080 due to climate change, incorporating the effects of carbon fertilization

-50%　　　　　-15%　　　0　　　+15%　　　+35%　　No data

**Figure 18: Projected losses in food production due to climate change by 2080.** (Source: Cline, 2007).

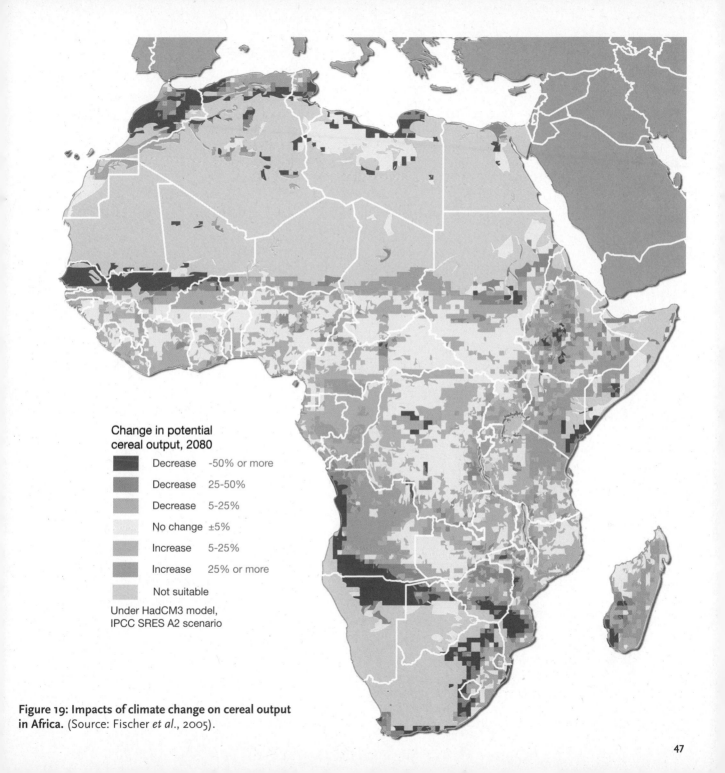

Change in potential
cereal output, 2080

Decrease   -50% or more
Decrease   25-50%
Decrease   5-25%
No change  ±5%
Increase   5-25%
Increase   25% or more
Not suitable

Under HadCM3 model,
IPCC SRES A2 scenario

**Figure 19: Impacts of climate change on cereal output in Africa.** (Source: Fischer *et al.*, 2005).

# IMPACTS OF WATER SCARCITY ON YIELD

Water is essential not only to survival but is also equally or even more important than nutrients in food production. Agriculture accounts for nearly 70% of the water consumption, with some estimates as high as 85% (Hanasaki *et al.*, 2008a,b). Water scarcity will affect over 1.8 billion people by 2025 (WHO, 2007). This could have major impacts on health, particularly in rural areas, and thus also major impacts on farmer productivity. Although of great significance, such indirect effects are not considered here. Current projections suggest that water demand is likely to double by 2050 (Figure 20). Estimates project water withdrawals to increase by 22–32% by 2025 (De Fraiture *et al.*, 2003) and nearly double by 2050, for all SRES scenarios (Shen *et al.*, 2008). For poor countries with rapid population growth and depletion of groundwater, water-deficit induced food insecurity is a growing problem (Rosegrant and Cai, 2002; Yang *et al.*, 2003). One major factor beyond agricultural, industrial and urban consumption of water is the destruction of watersheds and natural water towers, such as forests in watersheds and wetlands, which also serve as flood buffers (UNEP, 2005).

Studies of 128 major river basins and drainage regions show that approximately 20 to 50% of the mean annual river flow in different basins needs to be allocated to freshwater-dependent ecosystems in order to maintain them in good ecological condition. In large parts of Asia and North Africa and some parts of Australia, North America and Europe, current total direct water withdrawals (primarily for irrigation) already tap into the estimated environmental water requirements (Smakhtin *et al.*, 2004). The global consumption of both "blue" water (withdrawn for irrigation from rivers, lakes and aquifers) and "green" water (precipitation) by rainfed and irrigated agriculture and other terrestrial ecosystems is steadily rising (Rost *et al.*, 2008).

Water is probably one of the most limiting factors in increasing food production. Yields on irrigated croplands are, on average, 2–3 times higher than those on rainfed lands. Irrigated land currently produces 40% of the world's food on 17% of its land (FAO, 1999), most of it downstream and dependent upon glacial and snowmelt from the Hindu Kush Himalayas. It is evident that in regions where snow and glacial mass are the primary sources of water for irrigation, such as in Central Asia, parts of the Himalayas Hindu Kush, China, India, Pakistan and parts of the Andes, melting will eventually lead to dramatic declines in the water available for irrigation, and hence, food production (Figure 21).

The melting glaciers will impact certain countries more than others, and also substantially impact hydropower production. The Indus River and its tributaries, for example, in addition to providing nearly 60% of the water utilized for irrigation, also provide 45% of the electrical energy in Pakistan.

Of great importance, therefore, is the effect of climate change on the extent of snow and glacial mass (UNEP, 2007) and on the subsequent supply of water for irrigation. Climate change could seriously endanger the current food production potential, such as in the Greater Himalayas Hindu Kush region and in Central Asia (Figure 21). Currently, nearly 35% of the crop production in Afghanistan, Bangladesh, Bhutan, China, India, Myanmar, Nepal and Pakistan is based on irrigation, sustaining over 2.5 billion people. Here, water demand is projected to increase by at least 70–90% by 2050.

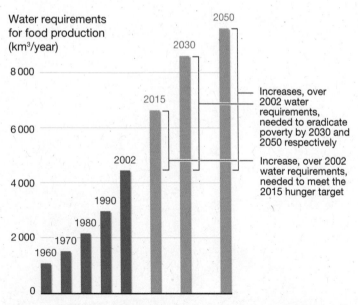

**Figure 20: Historic and projected changes in water consumption for food production, 1960-2050.** (Source: ).

This also includes supply to regions of Central Asia, China and Pakistan, which are under direct water stress today.

A decline of 10–30% in irrigated yields in the basins originating from the mountains of the Himalayas and Central Asia corresponds to 1.7–5.0% of the world cereal production (see box). A 10–30% yield loss due to lower availability of water for irrigation (without increased water efficiency) on the world's irrigated croplands would equate to losses in the range of 4–12% of world cereal production. In many regions, greater losses have already been observed due to over-extraction of water resources from aquifers and rivers. Studies suggest that almost half of the irrigation water comes from non-renewable

and non-local sources (Rost *et al.*, 2008). Indeed, river discharge is decreasing in many areas mainly as a result of anthropogenic use, particularly irrigation (Gerten *et al.*, 2008). Currently, an estimated 24% of the world river basin area has a withdrawal/availability ratio greater than 0.4, which some experts consider to be a rough indication of "severe water stress". Under a "business-as-usual" scenario of continuing demographic, economic and technological trends up to 2025, water withdrawals are expected to increase in 59% of world river basin area, outweighing the assumed improvements in water-use efficiency, although with great geographic variation (Alcamo *et al.*, 2003). On the assumption that the melting glaciers would cause reduced production by 2050, as indicated,

An impressive layer of ice covered Imja Glacier in the 1950s. Thick ice falls down from the mountain and the glacier merges with the Lhotse Shar glacier further down. However, even in the 1950s, small melt water ponds could be seen in and around the glacier. Over the next fifty years, these ponds continued to grow, merge, and by the mid 1970s had formed the Imja lake.

By 2006, the Imja lake was around 1 km² in size, with an average depth of 42 m, and contained more than 35 million m³ of water. The Imja Glacier is retreating at a rate of 74 m per year, and is thought to be the fastest retreating glacier in the Himalayas. The thin cover of debris on this glacier may actually have accelerated surface melting, as heat is transferred to the ice below. Because of the unconsolidated nature of the lake's terminal moraine dam, the risk of a glacial lake outburst flood (GLOF) may be high.

and that a similar estimate for the remaining irrigated lands is considered an upper estimate, then the range of reduced yields due to water scarcity is in the region of 1.7–12% of the projected yield by 2050. Given the high dependence on many of the world's rivers for irrigation, this estimate could be quite optimistic.

Except for the fact that glaciers are melting rapidly in many places, we do not have adequate data to more accurately project when and where water scarcity will affect irrigation schemes in full. Making accurate projections is also difficult because of variations in the effects on ground and surface water, as well

as on water for urban needs and industrial purposes Furthermore, the cost of water may also increase, seriously complicating the water scarcity question. Recent studies show that cost of water has increased by about 400–500% since 1990 in the Indo-Gangetic Basin of India.

Extreme weather events are also very hard to predict. Floods and particularly drought can offset production gains and create great fluxes in crop production, as well as in the survival of livestock. Indeed, a higher frequency of extreme weather events can have severe impacts on crop and livestock production, particularly in Africa that appears especially vulnerable

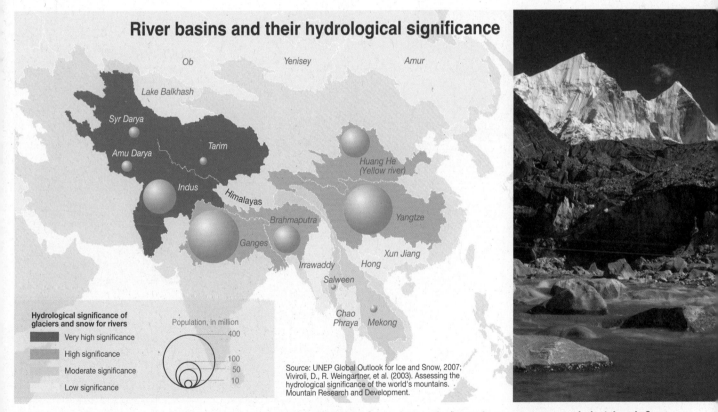

**Figure 21: Many of the largest rivers in the Himalayas Hindu Kush region are strongly dependent upon snow and glacial melt for waterflow.** Indeed, some scenarios suggest a 20–90% increase in annual flow due to glacial reduction, followed by a 10–40% decline, as glaciers and snow fall below critical thresholds for functions as water towers in 2050–2100. Combined with possible extreme precipitation events, this may result in greater seasonal droughts, and damage from floods. (Source: Rees and Collins, 2004; UNEP, 2007).

## Melting glaciers jeopardize Asian and world food production

Irrigated croplands, mainly rice, in the watersheds of the Indus, Ganges, Brahmaputra, Yangtze, Huang He (Yellow River), Tarim, Syr Darya and Amu Darya are all, to varying extents, dependent on glacial water and snowmelt from the mountains (Winiger *et al.*, 2005). With rising temperatures, combined with changes in the monsoon, up to 80% of the glaciated area may be lost within this century (Böhner and Lehmkuhl, 2005; UNEP, 2007).

While data are sparse in this region, actual observations from Nepal indicate that current warming at high altitudes is occurring much faster than the global average, up to 0.03° C per year (Shrestha, 1999), and even faster at higher altitudes, up to 0.06° C per year (Liu and Chen, 2000; Eriksson *et al.*, 2008). Scenarios suggest that the effects on the rivers are highly variable, ranging from a major increase in annual flow until around 2050 followed by a relatively rapid decline in flow for the Indus , to a gradual decline in flow in rivers such as the Brahmaputra. If temperatures rise quickly, such as >0.06° C per year, the annual flow of the rivers will invariably decline over time, particularly for those dependent on the mountains, but less so for those more dependent on the monsoons (UNEP, 2004; 2007).

The irrigated cropland in these basins, which are the most dependent upon the mountains for water flow, comprises approximately 857,830,000 ha (UNEP, 2005; 2008). If average production on irrigated rice is projected at 6 tonnes/ha (range 2–10 tonnes/ha), compared to 2–3 tonnes/ha for non-irrigated land (combined, average about 3.3 tonnes/ha in Asia), the water from the melting Himalayas annually supports the production of over 514 million tonnes of cereals, equivalent to nearly 55.5% of Asia's cereal production and 25% of the world production today. A reduction of, for example, 10–30% due to increased flood damage to irrigated lands combined with reduced water flow and seasonal drought, would thus lower world cereal production of 3,000 million tonnes (by 2050) by 1.7–5%, even if we assume no other yield increases in this period (in which case losses would be larger).

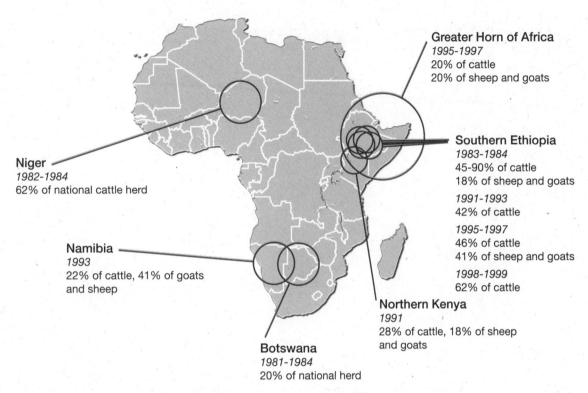

**Figure 22: Impacts on drought on livestock numbers in selected African countries.** (Source: IPCC, 2007).

to such events. For example, nine major droughts in selected African countries between 1981 and 2000 resulted in an average livestock loss of 40%, with a range of 22–90% (Figure 22). Similar effects may be observed on crop production. Based on the extent of irrigated cropland impacted in Asia and increasing water scarcity as a result of extreme weather, an annual reduction in the future from climate-induced water scarcity and decreasing water tables may account for an estimated reduction of the world food production by 1.5% by 2030 and at least 5% by 2050.

Water scarcity in terms of drought or depleted groundwater could therefore have great impacts on livestock and rangelands. These interactions are also complex. While drought can directly threaten livestock, other factors that influence water availability for livestock are seasonal droughts and socio-economic changes, such as permanent settlement and occupation of seasonal pastures by people other than pastoralists, availability and quality of rangelands, livestock numbers and management approaches.

The combined effects of melting of glaciers, seasonal floods and overuse of ground and surface water for industry, settlements and irrigation, combined with poor water-use efficiency are difficult to estimate. However, given that 40% of the world's crop yields are based on irrigation, and almost half of this from the basins of rivers originating in the Himalayas alone, the effect of water scarcity can be substantial.

# IMPACTS OF SPECIES INFESTATIONS ON YIELD

Invasive alien species (IAS) are now thought to be the second gravest threat to global biodiversity and ecosystems, after habitat destruction and degradation (Mooney *et al.*, 2000; CBD, 2001; Kenis *et al.*, 2009). The steady rise in the number of invasive alien species is predicted to continue under many future global biodiversity scenarios (Sala *et al.*, 2000; Gaston *et al*, 2003; MA, 2005), although environmental change could also cause non-alien species to become invasive. Environmental change (e.g., rising atmospheric $CO_2$, increased nitrogen deposition, habitat fragmentation and climate change) could promote further invasions (Macdonald, 1994; Malcolm *et al.*, 2002; Le Maitre *et al.*, 2004; Vilà *et al.*, 2006; Song *et al.*, 2008). As invasive or alien species comprise over 70% of all weeds in agriculture (estimated in the US) (Pimentel *et al.*, 2005), increases in invasive species pose a major threat to food production (Mack *et al.*, 2000; MA, 2005; Pimentel *et al.*, 2005; Chenje and Katerere, 2006; van Wilgen *et al.*, 2007).

In Australia, the varroa mite, a serious pest in honeybee hives, may result in the loss of $30 million a year in free pollination services from feral bees (CSIRO, 2008). The varroa mite has recently invaded New Zealand and is expected to have an economic cost of US$267–US$602 million, forcing beekeepers to alter the way they manage their hives (GISP, 2008). Invasive alien species such as pests and diseases also impose major constraints on world crop and livestock production (Oerke *et al.*, 1994). Pests and pathogens have had particularly severe effects on crop yields in the world's poorest and most food insecure region of Sub-Saharan Africa. They have been estimated to cause an annual loss of US$12.8 billion in yield of eight of Africa's principal crops, and may reduce yields in developing countries overall by around 50% (Oerke *et al.*, 1994).

Importantly, increased climate extremes may promote the spread of invasive species, plant diseases and pest outbreaks (Alig *et al.*, 2004; Anderson *et al.*, 2004; Gan, 2004; FAO, 2008). For instance, there is clear evidence that climate change is altering the distribution, incidence and intensity of animal and plant pests and diseases such as Bluetongue, a sheep disease that is moving north into more temperate zones of Europe (van Wuijckhuise *et al.*, 2006; FAO, 2008). According to FAO (2008), climate scenarios with more winter rain in the Sahel may provide better breeding conditions for migratory plant pests such as desert locust (*Schistocerca gregaria*) that are totally dependent on rain, temperature and vegetation, with catastrophic impacts on crop and livestock production.

People relying most directly on ecosystem services, such as small and subsistence farmers, the rural poor and traditional societies, face the most serious and immediate risks from IAS. These people depend

Worldwide 67,000 pest species attack crops: 9,000 insects and mites, 50,000 pathogens and 8,000 weeds. Up to 70% of them are introduced, with major impacts on global food production.

Across Africa, IAS of the genus *Striga* have a direct impact on local livelihoods: it affects more than 100 million people and as much as 40% of arable land in the savannahs. These invasive species stunt maize plant growth by attacking the roots and sucking nutrients and water, and thus in addition to the direct financial costs, have implications for food security (Chenje and Katerere, 2006).

Invasive alien species such as pests and diseases have been estimated to cause an annual loss of US$12.8 billion in yield of eight of Africa's principal crops (Oerke *et al.*, 1994).

In West Africa the larger grain borer (*Prostephanus truncates*), is responsible for cassava losses of approximately US$ 800 million per year thereby jeopardizing food security (Farrell and Schulten, 2002).

In Tanzania the larger grain borer (*Prostephanus truncates*) causes some US$ 91 million in maize losses per year (GISP, 2008).

Pimentel *et al.* (2001) estimated that crop losses due to introduced arthropods in South Africa amount to US$ 1.25 billion per year.

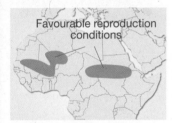

**July - September 2003**

Exceptional rains favour locust reproduction. Lack of funding for preventive intervention in the Sahel.

**October 2003 - February 2004**

Situation aggravated and start massive migration of destructive swarms.

**March - July 2004**

Massive reproduction in the Maghreb, limited reproduction in the Red Sea region. Invasion into the Sahel. Gregarious populations eradicated on the coast of the Red Sea.

**August - November 2004**

Monsoon creates favourable conditions for reproduction in West Africa. Massive and early migration of swarms born in the Sahel towards the Maghreb and eastward towards Egypt, Lebanon and Cyprus.

**Figure 23: A shift in desert locust (*Schistocerca gregaria*) host range due to climate change might have catastrophic impacts on food and livestock production.** According to UNICEF (2005) it is estimated that two-thirds of the 2004 loss in food production and pasture in Niger is rooted in the impact of drought at national level, while desert locusts, which infested the country afterwards, caused one-third of the overall damages. In certain areas, swarms of desert locusts consumed nearly 100% of the crops. The desert locust, like other locusts, can change its behaviour and physiology from solitary individuals to gregarious stages that form swarms. Solitary desert locusts occur at low density in the recession area, which covers North Africa, the Sahel, the Red Sea countries and parts of Afghanistan, India, Iran and Pakistan. The outbreak area stretches from Mauritania to India and from southern Europe to Cameroon and Tanzania. Outbreaks and plagues originate in the recession areas when there are several cycles of good breeding conditions. Although the effects of climate change on this system are difficult to judge, climate scenarios with more winter rain in the Sahel may provide better breeding conditions. Large amounts of chemicals are being used to stem this plague, at considerable risk to the environment and public health. A hazard is that locusts depend on the wind and rain to travel. (Source: CIRAD/UNEP/GRID-Arendal 2005).

on the safety net provided by natural ecosystems in terms of food security and sustained access to fuel, medicinal products, construction materials and protection from natural hazards such as storms and floods (MA, 2005). With the number of IAS in terrestrial ecosystems expected to increase, these impacts are likely to worsen and hamper efforts to meet the growing demands for food (FAO, 2008). In addition, they will likely be exacerbated further by climate change (Pyke *et al.*, 2008).

Alien invasive weeds and pathogens are estimated to be responsible for about 8.5% and 7.5% in yield reduction, respectively, equivalent to US$24 billion and US$21 billion of a crop value of US$267 billion (USBC, 2001; Pimentel *et al.*, 2004; Rossman, 2009). Different estimates range from US$1.1–US$55 billion in losses every year, corresponding to annual losses of 0.4% (OTA, 1993) to 17% (Pimentel *et al.*, 2004; 2005; Rossman, 2009). This does not include increased expenses for more mechanical or pesticide weed control or losses from invasive insects (about 5%) or diseases of livestock.

## Current and future global food crises may also facilitate the spread of invasive species

The spread of invasive species frequently occurs in the provision of humanitarian emergency food aid. Lower sanitary and phytosanitary standards apply to food aid, particularly emergency food aid, so it may not be surprising that the introduction and spread of potentially invasive species would follow the distribution of emergency relief. For example:

- The grey leaf spot (*Circosporda zeae-maydis*) is thought to have been introduced into Africa via US food aid shipments of maize during the 1980's (Ward *et al.*, 1999). It has subsequently spread into all the main maize-growing areas of Africa, and its effect on yields has been such that it is now argued to pose a serious threat to food security (Rangi, 2004).
- The parthenium weed (*Parthenium hysterophorus*) from Mexico arrived in Africa through grain shipments for famine relief to Ethiopia, where it has earned a local indigenous name which translates to "no crop" (Chenje and Katerere, 2006).

Therefore, the spread of plant pests, weeds and animal diseases across physical and political boundaries threatens food security and represents a global public "bad" that links all countries and all regions.

## Using crop genetic diversity to combat pests and diseases in agriculture

Each year farmers experience significant crop losses as a result of disease and pest infestation. These losses can be intensified by changes in climatic conditions. To cope with pest and disease problems, modern agriculture depends to a great extent on the use of pesticides and the continuing production of new crop varieties with specific resistance genes, although the value of integrated pest management techniques and biological control are increasingly recognized. Other ways of increasing productivity while reducing dependence on pesticides are essential for increasing productivity in sustainable ways.

Traditional crop varieties are a primary source of new resistant germplasm for both farmers and breeders. These crop varieties often contain a number of different resistance genes and resistance mechanisms against a range of pests and diseases. In many regions of the world, farmers have local preferences for growing mixtures of varieties, which they understand provide resistance to local pests and diseases and enhance yield stability. Within-crop diversity through the use of variety mixtures, multilines or the use of different varieties in the same production environment has been found to reduce disease incidence and increase productivity without the need for pesticides.

Small-scale farmers in developing countries continue to depend on local genetic diversity to maintain sustainable production and meet their livelihood needs. Loss of genetic choices, reflected as the loss of traditional crop varieties, therefore diminishes farmers' capacities to cope with changes in pest and disease infection, and leads to yield instability and loss. Intra-specific diversity can be used to reduce crop damage from pest and diseases today and for maintaining levels of diversity against future crop loss, that is, crop populations that have less probability that migrations of new pathogens or mutations of existing pathogens will damage the crop in the future.

In China, interplanting 2 varieties of rice has been found to have significant effects on disease incidence and productivity (Zhu *et al.*, 2000) and is now being used in 3 different provinces on thousands of hectares. A global project supported by UNEP and the Global Environment Facility is under way in China, Ecuador, Morocco and Uganda to develop ways in which farmers can use this approach to combat diseases in crops such as bananas, barley, faba beans and rice.

# IMPACTS OF ENVIRONMENTAL DEGRADATION ON FISHERIES

At present capture fisheries yield 110–130 million tonnes of seafood annually. Of this, 70 million tonnes are directly consumed by humans, 30 million tonnes are discarded and 30 million tonnes converted to fishmeal. Aquaculture, freshwater and marine fisheries supply about 10% of world human calorie intake – but this is likely to decline or at best stabilize in the future, and might have already reached the maximum.

The primary and most important fishing grounds are found along the continental shelves within less than 200 nautical miles of the shores. The distribution of these fishing grounds is patchy and very localized. Indeed, more than half of the 2004 marine landings were caught within 100 km of the coast in depths generally less than 200 m covering an area of less than 7.5% of the world's oceans, while 92% was caught in less than half of the total ocean area.

Climate change and increased $CO_2$ assimilation in the oceans will result in increasing ocean acidification, die-back of up to 80% of the world's coral reefs and disruption of thermohaline circulation and other processes. It will particularly impact dense-shelf water cascading, a "flushing" mechanism that helps to clean polluted coastal waters and carry nutrients to deeper areas. Coastal development is increasing rapidly and is projected to impact 91% of all inhabited coasts by 2050 and contribute to more than 80% of all marine pollution. Increased development, coastal pollution and climate change impacts on currents will accelerate the spreading of marine dead zones, many in or around primary fishing grounds (Diaz and Rosenberg, 2008).

Overfishing and bottom trawling are reducing fish stocks and degrading fish habitats, and threatening the entire productivity of ocean biodiversity hotspots, making them more vulnerable to climate change. Up to 80% of the world's primary fisheries stocks are exploited close to or beyond their optimum harvest capacity and large areas of productive seabeds on some fishing grounds have been partly or extensively damaged. For example, over 95% of the damage and change to seamounts has been caused by bottom trawling, which has been estimated to be as damaging to the seabed as all other fishing gear combined. Damaged from overfishing , bottom trawling and pollution, the worlds fishing grounds are increasingly becoming infested by invasive species mainly through ballast water, with the pattern closely following the major shipping routes.

The result of unsustainable fishing practices are that we might no longer able to increase the landings from conventional fisheries, and might, in fact, be facing a substantial decline in the world's fisheries in the coming decade. This will also have severe impacts on aquaculture production, which relies on fish for feed.

## AQUACULTURE

Aquaculture production has increased more than seven-fold in weight (from 5 to 36 million tonnes) between 1980 and 2000. The value generated has grown from US$9 billion in 1984 to US$52 billion in 2000 (Deutsch *et al.*, 2007). In 2006, the world consumed 110.4 million tonnes of fish, of which 51.7 million tonnes originated from aquaculture. In order to meet the growing fish demand, aquaculture will have to produce an additional 28.8 million tonnes – 80.5 million tonnes overall – each year, just to maintain per capita fish consumption at current levels. Aquaculture growth rate is declining, however: a yearly growth rate of 11.8% from 1985 to 1995 slowed to 7.1% during the following decade, and to 6.1% for the 2004–2006 period. In October 2008, FAO cautioned that a series of emerging challenges need to be addressed if aquaculture is to meet increasing demand for fish.

## THE FEED BOTTLENECK

Almost 40% of all aquaculture production is now directly dependent on commercial feed. Most farmed fish that are consumed in the developing world, such as carps and tilapia, are herbivores or omnivores. But other species like salmon or shrimp – often raised in developing countries – are fed other fish in the form of fishmeal or oil. Salmon, shrimp and trout aquaculture alone accounts for almost 50% of all fishmeal used in aquaculture, but provides less than 10% of the production volumes (Deutsch *et al.*, 2007). In 2006, aquaculture consumed 3.06 million tonnes (56%) of world fishmeal production and 780,000 tonnes (87%) of total fish oil production. Over 50% of the sector's use of fish oil occurs on salmon farms. Fishmeal and fish oil production has remained stagnant over the last decade and significant increases in their production are not

anticipated, according to FAO. At the same time, the volume of fishmeal and fish oil used in formulated aquaculture feeds tripled between 1996 and 2006. This was made possible by a significant reduction of the poultry sector's reliance on fishmeal for poultry feeds. As formulated feeds are increasingly being used for non-filter feeding omnivorous fish like carps, the demand for fishmeal is increasing.

As for meat production, feed is a major bottleneck. It is extremely difficult to project the future role of fisheries and aquaculture, but it is evident that the growth in aquaculture may be limited by access to feed, which, in turn is partly dependent on capture fish-eries. There is no indication that today's marine fisheries could sustain the 23% increase in landings needed to sustain the 56% growth in aquaculture production required to maintain per capita fish consumption at current levels. Given the grave nature of the trends and scenarios on overfishing and ocean degradation, a future collapse of ocean fisheries would immediately affect aquaculture production and the prices of aquaculture products. Even assuming that marine fisheries landings can be maintained at current levels, the proportion of fish in the diet (in terms of calorie intake) may go down from the current 2% of world human calorie intake to 1.5% by 2030 and to only 1% by 2050. This loss will have to be compensated for by either meat or crops.

# RANGES OF IMPACTS ON CROPLAND AREA AND YIELDS

The combined impact of reductions in yield and in the area available for food production will have to be compensated either by even further yield increases, cropland expansion, or by increasing food energy efficiency.

The extent of the impact of each individual factor on food production is likely to exhibit great regional variation. This probably also applies to the possible socio-economic responses, including that of policy changes as well as the responses and incentives for change of the individual farmer. It also applies to the financial and institutional capacity of the country, region and individual farm to cope with increasing stressors.

As the extent of interaction, synergistic or cumulative effects are not known, the projections should be interpreted cautiously, reflecting mainly a risk assessment and indication of the possible magnitude and relevance of environmental degradation for future food supply.

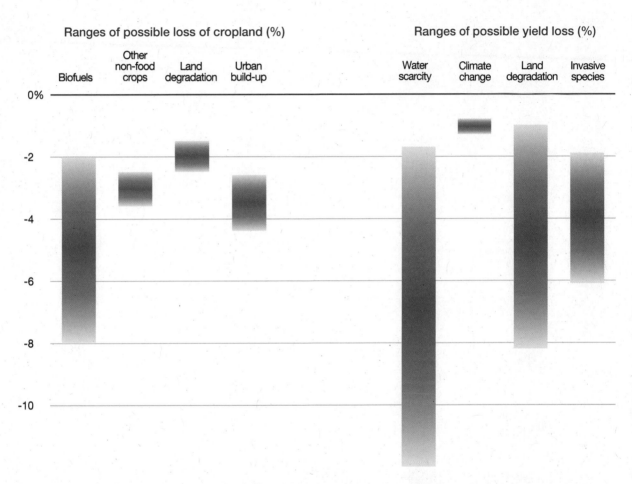

**Figure 24: Possible individual ranges of yield and cropland area losses by 2050** with climate change (A2 scenario), non-food crops incl. biofuels (six OECD scenarios), land degradation (on yield and area, respectively, see text), water scarcity (including gradual melt of Himalayas glaciers, see box and text) and pests (invasive species of weeds, pathogens and invertebrates such as insects, see text). Although these effects may be considerable, cumulative and indirect effects or interactions are not considered here, nor are the cumulative loss of ecosystems services endangering the entire functioning of food production systems. Notice that the climate impact bar only relates to changes in general growing conditions incl. temperature, evapotranspiration and rainfall, not the indirect impacts of climate change such as on glacial melt (water scarcity) and increases in invasive species. The other bars in part incorporate some of these important climate change impacts. Effects of extreme weather is not included, but could be substantial (Source: Compiled by UNEP for this report).

## Uncertainties in future scenarios

As defined by the FAO, food security exists when all people, at all times, have physical and economic access to sufficient, safe and nutritious food to meet their dietary needs and food preferences for an active and healthy life. Future food security depends on developments in both supply and demand, but projections for these variables are cursed with uncertainty. On the demand side, population and economic growth are particularly subject to a high degree of uncertainty. Key uncertainties for future supply have to go with agricultural productivity and energy markets. In addition, developments are contingent on new policies being put in place.

More specific causes of uncertainty in predicting future trends are:

- **Climate change:** While mean temperature changes are quite well modelled, rainfall changes and extreme weather events are much less so, particularly at smaller scales, neither are extreme weather conditions predictable today.

- **Energy supply:** If peak oil supply is reached within the period under consideration, this will have major consequences for the economics of virtually all aspects of food production as well as on likely demands for biofuels.

- **Technological advances in food production**, such as by the use of genetically modified crops may also influence yield projections.

- **Availability of freshwater** (linked with climate change and with technology).

- **Human behaviour:** Food preferences, ability to adapt to changing conditions for food supply, commitment to more equitable distribution of resources or increased tendency to defend local resource base. (Economic factors as major proximate driver of food production decisions: supply/demand curves, input costs, extent of exposure to international markets, government policy as expressed in subsidies, tariffs, etc).

- **Impacts of pests and diseases** (including alien invasive species) on food supply.

- **Actual versus predicted population growth.**

- **Major disease outbreaks in humans.**

- **Other catastrophic events** (war, major earthquakes, volcanic events, etc).

The future impact of some of these is so unpredictable that it is difficult to see how they can realistically be incorporated into any quantitative models, other than through including some essentially arbitrary tolerance limits in calculating necessary food supplies.

Overall, no fully integrated model currently exists that assesses agriculture in a holistic way. Current models and scenarios focus on one or very few of these areas, e.g., land use change (IMAGE model), global climate models (e.g., UK Met office model), or are add-ons to these models (e.g., GLOBIO biodiversity model) with feedbacks and interconnections not fully integrated.

# IMPACTS ON BIODIVERSITY AND ECOSYSTEMS FROM CONVENTIONAL EXPANSION OF FOOD PRODUCTION

The Earth's natural environment provides the platform upon which all life is based. Ecosystems provide regulating as well as supporting services that are essential for agriculture and fisheries. These include provisioning of food, fibre and water; regulating services such as air, water and climate regulation, pollination and pest control; and providing resilience against natural disasters and hazards. Despite its crucial role in providing food, agriculture remains the largest driver of genetic erosion, species loss and conversion of natural habitats. Globally, over 4,000 assessed plant and animal species are threatened by agricultural intensification, and the number is still rising. Over 1,000 (87%) of a total of 1,226 threatened bird species are impacted by agriculture. Overfishing and destructive fishing methods along with eutrophication caused by high nutrient run-off from agricultural areas are among the major threats to inland and marine fisheries.

If increase in food production is to be met only by indiscriminate expansion of cropland area, intensification of yields using artificial fertilizers and pesticides and by increasing harvest beyond sustainable levels, we may further erode the platform upon which food production is based. Finding alternatives to the use of cereal in animal feed, recycling of waste for feed and energy recovery, and reducing the use of croplands for non-food purposes will not only increase food energy efficiency in production, but will also greatly help to preserve biodiversity and other natural resources, and the human communities and cultures that they support.

# ECOSYSTEM SERVICES

Ecosystems have been described as the life support system of the Earth – for humans as well as all life on this planet (MA Health Synthesis Report 2005). Ecosystem services, the benefits that humans derive from ecosystems, are considered "free", often invisible, and are therefore not usually factored into decision-making. This chapter discusses the role of the diverse forms of living species – biodiversity – in food production, focusing on agriculture and marine capture fisheries, as these provide the bulk of global food production.

Agriculture (livestock and foodcrops) require a range of conditions for optimum productivity. These conditions are generated by natural ecological components and processes as well as through artificial enhancement.

Water resources for agriculture are highly dependent on natural ecosystems and biodiversity, in particular vegetation such as forests in terms of flow regulation. This is crucial for providing a dependable water supply to crop areas, such as through retention of water in wetlands and forests buffering both droughts and floods (Bruijnzeel, 2004; UNEP, 2005). At present 75% of

globally usable freshwater supplies comes from forested catchments (Fischlin et al., 2007), therefore water is critically linked to forests. These ecosystems also help buffer global climate change (Nepstad et al., 2007).

Genetic diversity plays a critical role in increasing and sustaining food production levels and nutritional diversity. Diverse organisms contributing to soil biodiversity perform a number of vital functions that regulate the soil ecosystem, including decomposition of litter and cycling of nutrients such as nitrogen. Crop rotations or agroforestry increase yield stability and soil fertility; grassland and pasture/crop systems tend to be more sustainable because they provide opportunities for rotation diversity. Biodiversity may create "pest suppressive" conditions and greater resistance to invasion of farming systems by noxious species. Pollinators are essential for the production of a large number of crops (e.g., cereal, orchard, horticultural and forage production), and contribute to improvements in quality of both fruit and fiber crops; this service is ensured by an abundance and diversity of pollinators, in large part provided by wild biodiversity.

Pest control is another key ecosystem service underpinned by biodiversity; it is greatly determined by the abundance of natural enemies of the pest species involved. Improved pest control is dependent on a diversity of natural enemies of pests, and non-crop habitats are fundamental for the presence and survival of these biological control agents (predators, parasitoids) (Zhang et al., 2007). Landscape diversity or complexity, and proximity to semi-natural habitats tend to produce a greater abundance and species richness of natural enemies (Bianchi et al., 2006; Kremen and Chaplin-Kramer 2007; Tscharntke et al., 2007; Balmford et al., 2008). Thus, the main threat to the provision of biological control as an ecosystem service seems to be habitat loss and degradation, now exacerbated by potentially disruptive climate change. Indeed, Balmford et al., (2008) suggest that there is a medium to high probability that the provisioning of biological control is subject to thresholds/tipping points in the foreseeable future (by 2025), particularly in regions of very intensively managed agriculture.

# ENVIRONMENTAL COSTS OF CONVENTIONAL INTENSIFICATION AND EXPANSION OF FOOD PRODUCTION

## EXPANSION OF CROP- AND RANGELANDS

Modern agricultural methods and technologies brought spectacular increases in food production (Tilman *et al.*, 2002), but not without high environmental costs. Efforts to boost food production, for example, through direct expansion of cropland and pastures, will negatively affect the capacity of ecosystems to support food production and to provide other essential services. Food production will undoubtedly be affected by external factors such as climate change, but the production and distribution of food is itself is also a major cause of climate change.

Despite its crucial role in feeding the world population, agriculture remains the largest driver of genetic erosion, species loss and conversion of natural habitats (MA, 2005). The conversion of natural habitats to cropland and other uses typically entails the replacement of systems rich in biodiversity with monocultures or systems poor in biodiversity. Large-scale agriculture brings ecosystem simplification and loss of (bio)diversity, thus reducing the potential to provide ecosystem services other than food production. Of some 270,000 known species of higher plants, about 10,000 –15,000 are ed-

ible and only about 7,000 are used in agriculture. However, globalization and agricultural intensification have diminished the varieties traditionally used, with only 30% of the available crop varieties dominating global agriculture. These, together with only 14 animals species, provide an estimated 90% of the world's consumed calories (FAO,1998).

Habitat modification through agriculture and a variety of other causes is, in general, the most important factor in increasing species' risk of extinction. Most of this habitat loss arises from encroaching farmland and habitat conversion for food and biofuel production (Figures 25, 26 and 27). Clearance for cropland or permanent pasture has reduced the extent of natural habitats on arable land by more than 50% (Green *et al.*, 2005), with much of the rest altered by temporary grazing (Groombridge and Jenkins, 2002). Habitat modification already affects more than 80% of the globally threatened mammals, birds and plants (Groombridge and Jenkins, 2002), with serious implications for ecosystem services and human wellbeing. Indeed, the most significant threat by far to the world's 5,500 mammal species

**Figure 25: A photographic impression of the gradual changes in two ecosystem types (landscape level) from highly natural ecosystems (90–100% mean abundance of the original species) to highly cultivated or deteriorated ecosystems (around 10% mean abundance of the original species).** Locally, this indicator can be perceived as a measure of naturalness, or conversely, of human-impact. (Source: CBD, 2008; Alkemade *et al.*, 2009).

is habitat loss, with over 2,000 (40%) species being negatively impacted (IUCN, 2008). Globally, over 4,000 of the assessed plant and animal species are threatened by agricultural intensification (IUCN, 2008). With continuing agricultural expansion, this number has increased to over 4,600 species, and is still rising. The IUCN Global Red List (IUCN, 2008) includes 457 of the globally assessed plants and animals that are threatened by agriculture in Sub-Saharan Africa. Of these, 65 are critically endangered and 182 endangered. Similarly, 683 species are threatened by agriculture in Latin America, of which 146 are critically endangered and 244 endangered.

Globally, over 1,000 (87%) of a total of 1,226 threatened bird species are impacted by agriculture. More than 70 species are affected by agricultural pollution, 27 of them seriously. Europe's farmland birds have declined by 48% in the past 26 years (European Bird Census Council, 2008). Pesticides and herbicides pose a threat to 37 threatened bird species globally (BirdLife, 2008), in addition to deleterious effects of agricultural chemicals on ground water (Bexfield, 2008).

Domesticated species diversity is also under threat. Worldwide, 6,500 breeds of domesticated mammals and birds are under immediate threat of extinction, reducing the genetic diversity for options in a changing environment (Diaz *et al.*, 2007; MA, 2005).

With the loss of biodiversity in both natural and agricultural systems comes the loss of other ecosystem services. In addition to food, fibre and water provisioning, regulating services such as air, water and climate regulation, water purification, pollination and pest control, as well as providing resilience against natural hazards and disasters and environmental change, are among the numerous examples of ecosystem services being lost under increasing intensification and expansion of agriculture.

## Loss of global biodiversity with unsustainable conventional expansion of cropland

A central component in preventing loss of biodiversity and ecosystem services, such as provisioning of water, from expanding agricultural production is to limit the trade-off between economic growth and biodiversity by stimulating agricultural productivity and more efficient land use. Further enhancement of agricultural productivity ('closing the yield gap') is the key factor in reducing the need for land and, consequently, the rate of biodiversity loss (CBD, 2008). This option should be implemented carefully in order to not cause additional undesired effects, such as emissions of excess nutrients and pesticides and land degradation. An increase in protected areas and change towards more eco-agricultural cropping systems and sustainable meat production could have immediate positive effects on both biodiversity and water resource management, while increasing revenues from tourism (CBD, 2008).

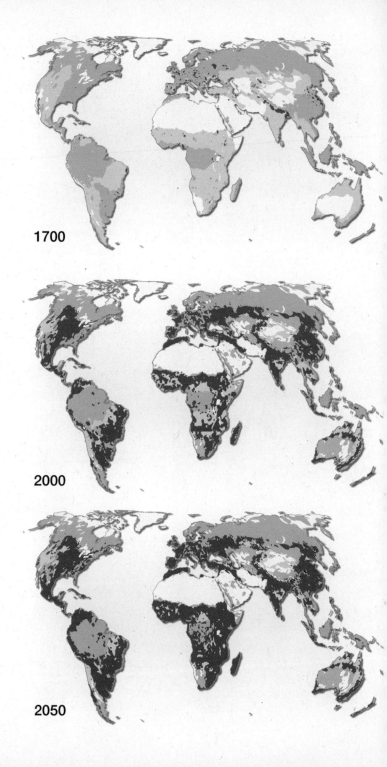

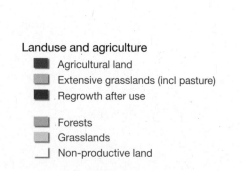

Landuse and agriculture
- ■ Agricultural land
- □ Extensive grasslands (incl pasture)
- ■ Regrowth after use

- ■ Forests
- □ Grasslands
- ⌐ Non-productive land

**Figure 26: Projected land use changes, 1700–2050.** (Source: IMAGE).

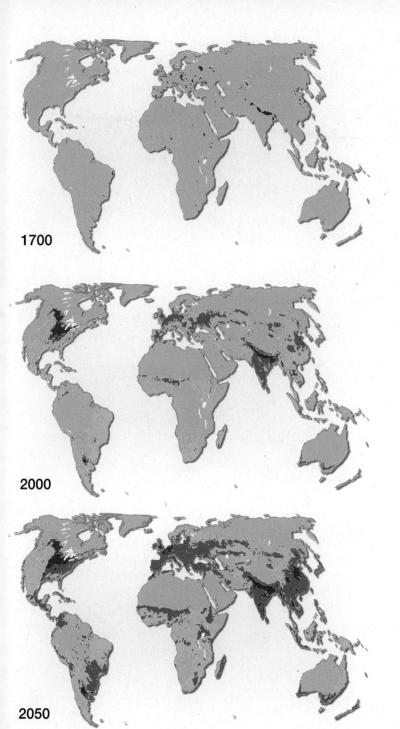

1700

2000

2050

Biodiversity, as ratio of species abundance before human impacts

| | | |
|---|---|---|
| ■ High impacts | 0 - 25 |
| ■ High-medium impacts | 25 - 50 |
| ■ Medium-low impacts | 50 - 75 |
| □ Low impacts | 75 - 100 % |

Mean species abundance (%)

**Figure 27: Loss of biodiversity with continued agricultural expansion, pollution, climate change and infrastructure development.** (Source: GLOBIO; Alkemade *et al.*, 2009).

# IMPACTS FROM INTENSIFICATION OF CROPLANDS

Intensive management to increase agricultural production – through irrigation and the application of fertilizers and pesticides – can further reduce the wildlife value of farmed land. From 1961 to 1999, the area of land under irrigation nearly doubled; the use of nitrogenous and phosphate fertilizers increased by 638% and 203%, respectively, and the production of pesticides increased by 854% (Green *et al.*, 2005). Such intensification has had major direct impacts on biodiversity, such as on farmland birds (Figure 28) and aquatic species. Large-scale use of fertilizers and pesticides, coupled with fragmentation and losses of important farmland habitat qualities, also reduces the number of flowers and plant diversity, diminishes insect biodiversity, and subsequently the survival of farmland birds, particularly the young that are dependent upon insects in their first weeks or months of life (see box).

Aquatic ecosystems are also being widely affected by food production in terrestrial areas, through high nutrient inputs (Seitzinger and Lee, 2008) in run-off from agricultural and livestock production and alteration of freshwater flows. The ensuing reduction in water quality (Mitchell *et al.*, 2005) is evident in increased eutrophication and subsequent algal blooms and oxygen-deficient waters, which when extreme, could result in dead zones (UNEP, 2001; 2008). In the northwestern Gulf of Mexico, nutrient enrichment mainly from fertilizer use in the Mississippi Basin has accounted for the world's largest hypoxic or dead zone (Turner and Rabalais 1991; Rabalais *et al.*, 1999; UNEP, 2008). Without significant nitrogen mitigation efforts, marine areas will be subjected to increasing hypoxia and harmful algal blooms that will further degrade marine biomass and biological diversity (Sherman and Hempel, 2008; UNEP, 2008).

In some regions, diversion of water for agricultural and other purposes has reduced river flow to coastal areas, with severe impacts on coastal habitats and estuarine-dependent species. For example, damming of the Colorado River has drastically changed what used to be an estuarine system into one of high salinity and reduced critical nursery grounds for many commercially important species, including shrimp (Aragón-Noriega and Calderon-Aguilera, 2000). There are many well-documented examples where diversion of water for agriculture has degraded and reduced the extent of inland water bodies (e.g., the Aral Sea), affecting fish spawning and migration and causing a collapse of the fishing industry and a loss of species diversity in the affected areas (MA, 2005).

## Loss of European Birds with agricultural intensification

Europe's common farmland birds declined severely during the past 26 years. Their average breeding populations in 2006 were about 50% lower than in 1980, and there is no sign of recovery. Farmland birds have suffered most in western Europe, which has the longest history of agricultural intensification. The countries of central and eastern Europe, which joined the European Union (EU) more recently (in 2004 or 2007), have not yet sustained such large losses of farmland birds, but their numbers are declining and are already much lower than in the 1980s. Agricultural intensification, such as the loss of crop diversity, destruction of grasslands and hedgerows, and excessive use of pesticides and fertilizers, has been widely recognised as one of the main driving forces behind this dramatic decline of common farmland birds. A transformation of the EU Common Agricultural Policy into a sustainable land management and rural development policy, thereby stopping the distribution of environmentally harmful subsidies, may prevent further declines of farmland bird populations.

Population index of common birds (1980=100)

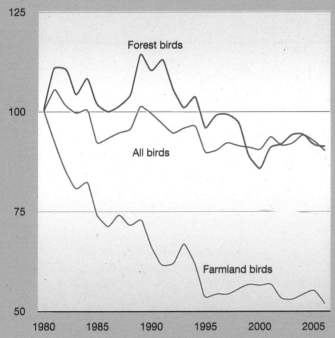

**Figure 28: Farmland birds in Europe have declined dramatically in the last decades, mainly as a result of agricultural intensification.** (Source: RSPB, European Bird Census Council (EBCC) and the Pan-European Common Bird Monitoring Scheme (PECBMS).

## Enhancing sustainability through the use of crop wild relatives

Crop wild relatives (CWR) – species or other taxa more or less closely related to crops, which include most of the progenitors of our domesticated types – have made a very significant contribution to modern agricultural production through the characteristics that they have contributed to plant cultivars.

Over the last 100 years, crop wild relatives have become increasingly important as sources of useful genes. For example, they have contributed resistance to pest and disease (e.g,. resistance to late blight in potato and grassy stunt virus in rice, which came from a single accession of Oryza nivara found in Orissa, India) and to abiotic stress. They have also increased nutritional values such as protein and vitamin content. The economic returns from investment in CWR can be striking; for example, genetic material from a tomato wild relative has allowed plant breeders to boost the level of solids in commercial varieties by 2.4%, which is worth US$250 million annually to processors in California alone (FAO, 1998).

The natural populations of many crop wild relatives are increasingly at risk, mainly from habitat loss, degradation and fragmentation. Moreover, the increasing industrialization of agriculture is reducing populations of crop wild relatives in and around farms. They are often missed by conservation programmes, falling between the efforts of agricultural and environmental conservation actions. A major global effort, coordinated by Bioversity International and supported by UNEP GEF, to find ways of securing the improved conservation of crop wild relatives is in progress in 5 countries (Armenia, Bolivia, Madagascar, Sri Lanka and Uzbekistan) in collaboration with a number of international agencies (FAO, UNEP-WCMC, IUCN and Botanic Gardens Conservation International – BGCI)

With current scenarios from the CBD, all regions of the world will continue to experience loss in biodiversity, with Africa, followed by Latin America and the Caribbean, experiencing the highest losses as a result of major land use changes (especially in increases in pastures and biofuel production) combined with increasing land degradation. Large areas of Africa are projected to lose more than 25% of mean species abundance by 2050 (UNEP, 2007). According to FAO's Global Perspective Unit (2008), at present 228 million ha of arable land are in use in Sub-Saharan Africa. Potentially, this area can be increased to over 1 billion ha of suitable land for rainfed crops in Africa by 2030. Likewise, in South America similar scenarios project the present 208 million ha in agricultural use to be increased to over 1 billion ha by 2030 at the expense of natural ecosystems. These expansions will have huge costs to biodiversity.

# FROM SUPPLY TO FOOD SECURITY

Food security is not simply a function of production or supply, but of availability, accessibility, stability of supply, affordability and the quality and safety of food. These factors include a broad spectrum of socio-economic issues with great influence on farmers and on the impoverished in particular.

Large shares of the world's small-scale farmers, particularly in central Asia and in Africa, are constrained by access to markets, while inputs, such as fertilizers and seed, are expensive. With lack of irrigation water, infrastructure and investments, and low availability of micro-finance combined with dependency on few multinational suppliers, crop production is unlikely to increase in those regions where it is needed the most, unless major policy changes and investments take place. These constraints are further compounded by conflicts and corruption.

Agricultural prices are forecast to decline over the next two years but to remain well above the levels of the first half of this decade. However, by 2030–2050, the current scenarios of losses and constraints due to climate change and environmental degradation – with no policy change – suggest that production increases could fall to 0.87% towards 2030 and to 0.5% by 2030–2050. Should global agricultural productivity rise by less than 1.2% per year on average, then prices, rather than declining, can be expected to rise by as much as 0.3% per year. In addition, a production short of demand, a greater geographical inequity in production and demand, combined with possibly more extreme weather and subsequent speculation in food markets, could generate much greater price volatility than before. In turn, this could potentially induce a substantially greater reduction in food security than that seen in the current crisis, if appropriate options for increasing supply and security are not considered and implemented.

The previous chapters clearly outlined the potential impact of environmental considerations on projected food demand and supply. These environmental considerations are not well addressed in global food assessments to date. Whether the Millennium Development Goals (MDGs) like hunger eradication will be met in the (near) future and whether the food crisis as evolved until 2008 will impact these MDGs on the longer term, depends on how markets will respond, how price impacts will cascade through the food production system and how international governments will respond to these new circumstances. In short, the impact on food availability and food security can only be assessed through the different dimensions that play a role in the state of food security. The FAO defines food security as follows: "Food security exists when all people, at all times, have physical and economic access to sufficient, safe and nutritious food for a healthy and active life" (FAO, 2003). This involves four dimensions:

- Adequacy of food supply or *availability*;
- *Stability* of supply, without seasonal fluctuations or shortages;
- *Accessibility* to food or affordability; and
- *Utilization*: quality and safety of food.

Before conclusions can be drawn on food security, these dimensions need to be examined. The first three dimensions are elaborated upon in this chapter. The fourth dimension of food utilization is beyond the scope of this report, of which the focus is the environmental aspects of food security.

# AVAILABILITY OF FOOD

The availability of food within a specific country can be guaranteed in two ways: Either by food production in the country itself or by trade. The first option has been discussed extensively in the previous chapters. The second option has become more and more important (Figure 29), with increasing transport possibilities and storing capacities and the growing challenges faced by some countries in their domestic production, including because of limitations in available cropland. International trade in agricultural products has expanded more rapidly than global agricultural GDP (FAO, 2005).

The past several decades have witnessed a major increase in the integration of the world economy through trade. Many parts of the world have experienced high economic growth in recent years. For example, Asia's GDP has increased by 9% annually between 2004 and 2006, and growth is especially high in China and India. Sub-Saharan Africa experienced 6% annual growth in the same period, after a long period of recession in many countries. Even countries with a prevalence of hunger reported some economic growth, although this is not always reflected in social conditions. However, global eco-

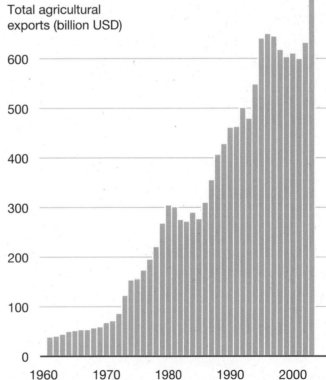

**Figure 29: World cereal trade in agriculture has increased steadily in the past decades.** OECD has always been the major net exporter and Asia has become a major net importer. (Source: FAOSTAT, 2009).

nomic growth is projected to slow to around 4% and be in the 6% range for developing countries beyond 2008 (IFPRI, 2008).

An increasing share of global agricultural exports originates from developed countries. It increased from 32% in 2000 to 37% in 2006, but there are large regional variations. For instance, Africa's share in global exports only increased from 2.3 to 2.8% in this period (UNCTAD, 2007). The EU countries account for most of the global growth; their share of total agricultural exports has increased from slightly more than 20% in the early 1960s to more than 40% today.

A large portion of this increase is accounted for by intra-EU trade, which represents around 30% of world agricultural trade. Conversely, during the past four decades, developing countries have seen their share of world agricultural exports decline from almost 40% to around 25% in the early 1990s before rebounding to about 30% today. This contrasts with the steadily increasing share of developing countries in total merchandise exports. Over this same period, the share of global agricultural imports purchased by developing countries increased from less than 20% to about 30% (FAO, 2005).

Another perspective of this trade is the purchase of land abroad for food production. Responding to recent food crises, a number of countries have started to purchase land abroad for cultivation of crops needed to support domestic demand (Figure 30). This is seen as a long-term solution to the high prices of agriculture commodities and increasing demand for agroforestry products such as palm oil. Among the most active countries owning, leasing or concessioning farmland overseas are China, India, Japan, Saudi Arabia, South Korea and United Arab Emirates; a number of other countries are only starting negotiations for the coming years. The total area of overseas farmland in different countries was estimated at 5.7 million ha at the end of 2008 or 0.4% of the global cropland area.

## INCREASING FOOD PRODUCTION

Another option for meeting food demand is to ensure production in the country or region itself, by aiming at self-sufficiency and lowering the dependency on other regions. Current estimates of the developments on the demand side require increase in production in those regions with the highest economic growth or population increase (see Chapter 2). The majority of these regions will be in emerging economies in Africa and

Asia. Nowadays, Africa is especially dependent on food imports. Food production in this region is lagging behind due to limited research investments and the problems for farmers to use the appropriate inputs in their production process.

## RESEARCH INVESTMENTS

The world regions are sharply divided in terms of their capacity to use science in promoting agricultural productivity in order to achieve food security and reduce poverty and hunger. For every US$100 of agricultural output, developed countries spend US$2.16 on public agricultural research and development (R&D), whereas developing countries spend only US$0.55 (IF-PRI, 2008). Total agricultural R&D spending in developing countries increased from US$3.7 billion (1991) to US$4.4 billion (2000), or by 1.6% annually (IFPRI, 2008). This spending was largely driven by Asia, where annual spending increased by 3.3 percent. Today, Asia accounts for 42% of total agricultural R&D spending in developing countries (with China and India accounting for 18 and 10%, respectively). In Africa, agricultural R&D expenditure declined slightly, by 0.4%/year. Although Af-

rica is geographically large, its share in R&D spending is only 13%. Latin America accounts for 33% (with Brazil being responsible for 48% of the region's spending).

Productivity has risen in many developing countries, mainly as a result of investment in agricultural R&D combined with improved human capital and rural infrastructure. In East Asia, land productivity increased from US$1,485/ha in 1992 to US$2,129/ha in 2006, while labour productivity rose from US$510 to US$822/worker. In Africa, the levels of productivity are much lower and their growth has also been slower. In 1992, land productivity in Sub-Saharan Africa was only 79% of that in East Asia; by 2006 this gap of 21% had increased to 59% (IFPRI, 2008).

## RESOURCES FOR FERTILIZER USE

One of the major options for significantly raising crop production is increasing the use of mineral fertilizers. The Africa Fertilizer Summit 2006 concluded that the use of fertilizers should be increased to a level of at least 50 kg/ha by 2015. The present use of fertilizers in Sub-Saharan Africa is only

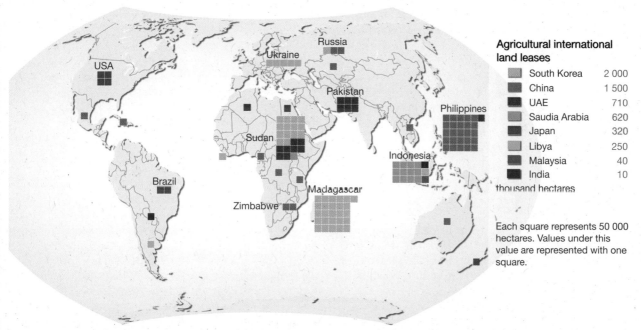

**Agricultural international land leases**

| | | |
|---|---|---|
| | South Korea | 2 000 |
| | China | 1 500 |
| | UAE | 710 |
| | Saudia Arabia | 620 |
| | Japan | 320 |
| | Libya | 250 |
| | Malaysia | 40 |
| | India | 10 |

thousand hectares

Each square represents 50 000 hectares. Values under this value are represented with one square.

**Figure 30: An increasing number of countries are leasing land abroad to sustain and secure their food production.** Data are preliminary only. (Source: GRAIN, 2008; Mongabay 2008).

about 9 kg/ha of arable land, compared to a world average of 101 kg/ha (Camara and Heinemaan, 2006; FAOSTAT 2009). Within Africa, there are strong differences in fertilizer use between regions, with relatively high use in Northern and Southern Africa, and very low use (around 1 to 2 kg/ha) in Western and Central Africa. Taking the increase as proposed by the Africa Fertilizer Summit as a starting point, this would mean a growth of the yearly use of fertilizers from 1 to 6 million tonnes. Based on the price of fertilizer (DAP) of approximately US$600/tonne (beginning of 2008), this would mean US$3 billion/year for the purchase of DAP only. A more moderate price of US$200/tonne would still mean US$1 billion/year. Added to this are significant costs of and investments in transport and distribution, developing agricultural research, extension programs, capacity building, etc. Indeed, there are many reasons for this low use. One of the reasons is the high retail prices of fertilizers, especially in areas with poor infrastructure. A metric tonne of urea costs $90 in Europe, $120 kg in the harbor of Mombassa, $400 in Western Kenya and $770 in Malawi (Sanchez, 2002).

A major challenge is to find ways of making fertilizer available to smallholders at affordable prices. There is also a need for holistic approaches to soil fertility management that embraces the full range of driving factors and consequences of soil degradation (TSBF-CIAT, 2006). This would include the integration of mineral and organic sources of nutrients, thereby using locally available sources of inputs and maximizing their use efficiency, while reducing dependency upon prices of commercial fertilizers and pesticides. The use of perennials, intercropping and agroforestry systems, such as the use of nitrogen fixating leguminous trees, are ways to increase nutrient availability, but also enhance water availability and pest control, in a more sustainable manner (Sanchez, 2002).

A major challenge is to find ways of making fertilizer available to smallholders at affordable prices. There is also a need for holistic approaches to soil fertility management that embraces the full range of driving factors and consequences of soil degradation (TSBF-CIAT, 2006). This would include the integration of mineral and organic sources of nutrients, thereby using locally available sources of inputs and maximizing their use efficiency.

## RESOURCES FOR IRRIGATION

Irrigated land area increased rapidly until 1980 with expansion rates of more than 2% a year. In Asia in particular, it led to a steady increase of staple food production together with other elements of the green revolution package (Faures et al., 2007). After 1980, growth in expansion of irrigated area decreased and it is assumed this trend will continue in the near future. One of the reasons is that the areas most suitable for irrigation are already used, leading to higher construction costs in new areas (Faures et al., 2007). Another reason is the strong decline in relative food prices over the last decades, which makes it less profitable to invest in irrigation. Current irrigation systems could be improved by investing in water control and delivery, automation, monitoring and staff training.

The irrigated area has remained very low in Sub-Saharan Africa and of the land under irrigation, 18% is not used (FAO, 2005b). In most African regions the major challenge is not the lack of water, but unpredictable and highly variable rainfall patterns with occurrences of dry spells every two years causing crop failure. This high uncertainty and variability drive the risk-averse behaviour of smallholder farmers. Rarely are investments made in soil management and fertility, crop varieties, tillage practices and even labour in order to avoid losses in case of total crop failure (Rockstrom et al., 2007a,b). Managing the extreme rainfall variability over time and space can provide supplemental irrigation water to overcome dry periods and prevent crop failure. In combination with improved soil management (in regions with severe land degradation, only 5% of the rainwater is used for crops), this should reduce the risk of total crop failure and enhance the profitability of investments in crop management, for example, fertilizers, labour and crop varieties. Increasing crop canopy coverage reduces evapo-transpiration from the soil, improving soil moisture and the provision of water for the crop.

# STABILITY OF FOOD SUPPLY

The second dimension of food security is the stability of food supply. Temporary disruption of supplies can have long-term impacts. The two options for fulfilling demand – food imports and domestic production – imply several reasons for instability of food supplies. A major reason for instability in food supply is high fluctuation in food prices (price volatility). Volatile prices lead to poor investment strategies of producers and immediate impacts on consumers, especially in developing countries where consumers spend a large share of their income on food. Another source of instability is conflicts, which increase food supply risks.

## PRICE VOLATILITY

Low and fluctuating prices are a core problem for stable food production. Agricultural price volatility increases the uncertainty faced by farmers and affects their investment decisions, productivity and income. Lagging investments can be a constraint in meeting changing consumer demands. For willingness to invest it is the volatility of the revenue flows that matters. Instability in prices is related to factors in the agricultural domain as well as in other sectors.

Trade policies that limit market access, increase the volatility of commodity prices, unfairly subsidize developed country exports and constrain the trade policy flexibility of the developing world affect the stability and security as well as overall economic wellbeing of developing countries. A quarter of the world's governments implemented some export restrictions in the current period of high prices to ensure domestic food security. The impacts of these restrictions varied from panic-buying to the cultivation of smaller areas due to high input costs and the expectation of low product prices. These restrictions even increased price volatility of food products on the world market, thereby decreasing the food security of other countries (FAO, 2008). Earlier experience shows that attempts to gain domestic price stability create global price instability (OECD, 2008; World Bank, 2008). Furthermore, once policies are established to protect food markets, they are not easily dismantled.

It should also be noted that global food prices are determined by a small share of food products that are traded on the global market. The share of cereals traded compared to the volume produced is small and has increased slightly over the last four decades, from 9% to 13%. Annual fluctuations in world cereal production are in the same order of magnitude, varying from +9.8% to –3.9% of the previous year's production. This implies that supplies to the world market (the sum of the surplus in the supply of each region) can be reduced by one-third or increase two-fold. Demand in the world market does not follow this trend, however, and probably even moves in the opposite direction in case of poor harvests. These yearly trends describe the risk of discrepancy between supply and demand on the world food market. For this reason, with open markets, developing countries are very vulnerable to fluctuations in global food supply and prices and temporary protection of their own agricultural markets is promoted for these countries.

Supplies from food stocks can also buffer shortages on the world market (FAO, 2008). Stocks of cereals and vegetable oil have fallen to low levels relative to use, reducing the buffer against shocks in supply and demand. Stocks are not expected to be fully replenished over the coming 10

years, implying that tight markets may be a permanent factor in the next decade. This does not necessarily lead to permanent higher prices, but provides the background for continuing price volatility in the future.

## CONSTRAINTS BY CONFLICTS

Conflicts increase the risk of food supply instability tremendously (Figure 31). Countries in conflict and post-conflict situations tend to be food insecure, with more than 20% of the population, and in many cases far more, lacking access to adequate food (IFPRI, 2006). The group of countries that are experiencing civil conflicts cannot meet their basic needs and are large importers of food. In addition, the transport of commodities is hazardous and the situation is not secure enough for farmers to make investment decisions.

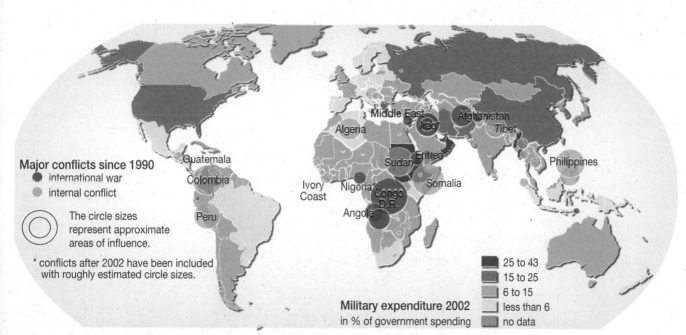

**Figure 31: Crushed by war and world conflicts.** For people in countries at war or subject to economic embargos, many goods are scarce, with shortages of food and water being the most crucial. (Source: PRIO, 2004).

# ACCESSIBILITY TO FOOD

Accessibility to food concerns both physical access and affordability. Access to markets concerns transportation of commodities and its costs as well as the transmission of price developments to producers. Poor transmission of price incentives to producers results in broadening the gap between consumers and producers, especially in periods of changing diets.

## ACCESS TO MARKETS

According to the latest UN estimates, almost all of the world's population growth between 2000 and 2030 will be concentrated in urban areas in developing countries (Figure 32). By 2030, almost 60% of the people in developing countries will live in cities (FAO, 2003). If present trends continue, urban population will equal rural population by around 2017.

Large urban markets create the scope for the establishment of big supermarket chains, with implications for the entire food supply chain. In 2002, the share of supermarkets in the processed/packaged food retail market was 33% in Southeast Asia and 63% in East Asia (Figure 33). The share of supermarkets in the fresh foods market was roughly 15–20% in Southeast Asia and 30% in East Asia outside of China. The 2001 supermarket share of Chinese urban food markets was 48%, up from 30% in 1999. Supermarkets are also becoming an emerging force in South Asia, particularly in urban India since the mid-1990s (Pingali and Khwaja, 2004).

The increasing growth and power of international food corporations are affecting the opportunities of small agricultural producers in developing countries. While new opportunities are being created, the majority are not able to utilize them because of the stringent safety and quality standards of food retailers, hence barring market entry. The economy of the corporate food supply chain has grown steadily over the past years. Between 2004 and 2006 total global food spend-

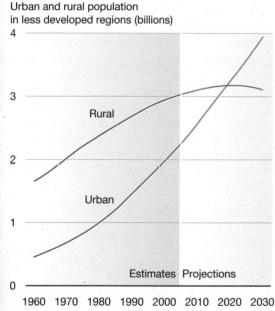

**Figure 32: Urbanization in developing countries between 1960 and 2030.** (Source: UN, 2007).

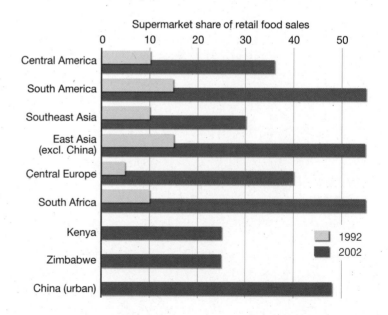

**Figure 33: Supermarket share of retail food sales.** (Source: Reardon et al., 2003).

ing grew by 16% from US$5.5 to US$6.4 trillion. In this period, the sales of food retailers increased disproportionately to the sales of food processors and companies in the food input industry. The sales of top food processors and traders grew by 13%, sales by the top 10 agricultural input countries by 8%, while the sales by top food retailers grew by 40% (IFPRI, 2007). However, on a global scale the agricultural input industry is more monopolized than the food retail industry. In the agricultural input industry, three agro-chemical corporations control approximately half the world market (UNCTAD, 2006), while the top five food retailers control only around 13% of the total market.

Trade and urbanization affect consumer preferences. The rapid diversification of the urban diet cannot be met by the traditional food supply chain in the hinterland of many developing countries. Consequently, importing food to satisfy the changing food demand could be relatively easier and less costly than acquiring the same food from domestic sources.

In Asia traditional rice-eating societies are consuming increasing quantities of wheat in the form of bread, cakes, pastry and other products (Pingali and Rosegrant, 1998). Countries that

traditionally imported rice for meeting food shortfalls may now be shifting towards increasing levels of wheat imports (Pingali, 2004). This trend is also evident in the import of other temperate products like vegetables, milk and dairy products and temperate fruit. Net imports of this category of products increased by a factor of 13 over the last 40 years, rising from a deficit of US$1.7 billion in 1961/1963 to US$24 billion in 1997/1999 (Pingali, 2004). Between 1997/1999 and 2030, the cumulative increase in imports of these products is expected to be 154% and 17% for vegetable oils and oilseeds, while meat imports are expected to increase by 389%. The overall result is that we are beginning to see a homogenization of food tastes across the globe, but with regional variations (Pingali, 2004).

Poor connections between urban and rural areas hinder price transmissions towards local markets, broadening the gap between urban demand and rural production in increasing demand for traditional products or for product diversification. The lack of access to markets is most evident in Africa, although large parts of Latin America and Asia are also experiencing long transport hours to reach markets (Figure 34). Consequently, do-

**Market access (agricultural areas)**

Less than 1 hour
1 - 2
2 - 5
5 - 10
More than 10 hours

Estimated travel time to nearest settlement of over 5000 people or more.

**Figure 34: Market access in agricultural areas of Africa, Asia and Latin America.** (Source: Sebastian, 2007).

mestic prices do not always follow international prices (FAO, 2006). The periods of rising real prices were generally associated with real exchange rate devaluations. Relaxation of government controls over prices and market systems also led to gains in producer prices in some cases. In other instances, import liberalization appears to have contributed to a decline in the real domestic prices of some commodities. Consequently, global shortages of food and feed that lead to global price increases are not followed by production increases at the local level.

## FUTURE WORLD FOOD PRICES

Accessibility to food is also determined by the long-term trend in food prices (which is a different issue from price volatility). The rising trend in global food prices is likely to persist in the next decade. In the long run, however, prices will decline (OECD-FAO, 2008).

Prices are driven by a complex combination of factors. Historically, productivity gains and increasing competition in trade have overtaken stronger demand, resulting in the declining trend of the past 100 years. Recently, food prices have been driven by a combination of rising fuel costs, production of biofuels, and unfavorable weather conditions, with trade restrictions boosting upward price pressures (World Bank, 2008).

Agricultural prices are forecast to decline over the next two years, but remain well above the levels of the first half of this decade. A strong combination of supply response and continued growth in demand is expected to keep prices above historical levels, but well below the peaks experienced in recent years (OECD-FAO, 2008). In real terms, prices in 2017 are projected to be 10% to 35% higher than in the past decade (OECD, 2008). While the long-term outlook for agricultural prices is particularly uncertain, the decline is expected to continue. In Global Economic Prospects, the World Bank projects a decline of about 0.7% a year through the forecast period until 2030 (World Bank, 2008b).

Price projections depend on a wide range of factors, including climate change, productivity developments, GDP and population growth and the policy environment. One of the cruel ironies today is seen in the connection between rising energy and food prices. Higher energy prices have increased fertilizer and

## The relationship between food prices and the oil price

# FERTILIZERS

Energy and agricultural commodity prices are increasingly correlated with each other. Rising oil prices increase fertilizer costs and freight rates. The emerging biofuel market strengthens these interdependencies, while a higher oil price increases demand for biofuels. The agricultural commodities used nowadays for biofuels were previously used for feed and fodder. As well demand for agricultural commodities as for factor inputs increases in this case.

Yields must increase by at least 43% by 2030 to meet demand, assuming all other factors constant (FAO, 2003). Fertilizer alone accounts for about 50% of historical increases in production (FAO, 2003). The projected increases required to sustain demand assume a substantial increase in the use of fertilizers by small-scale farmers in the region. As the cost of fertilizer is strongly correlated with oil prices, the future prices of oil will have a great influence on the accessibility of farmers to commercial fertilizer. Current FAO projections (2015/2030) scenario assumed an average oil price of US$21/barrel, while the later 2030/2050 scenario assumed an average oil price of US$53.4/barrel. At the peak of the current food crisis, oil prices hit US$147/barrel. As the cost, and subsequent use, of fertilizer is strongly correlated with price, a potentially higher oil price would lower the use of fertilizer or further increase the food price.

Fuel price is one of the main determining factors for fisheries. Rising energy prices have a strong impact on capture as well as aquaculture (for the production and transport of fish feed) and lead to higher costs during the processing, transport (particularly air freight) and distribution of fish products. Small-scale fisheries, which depend on outboard motors and small diesel engines, have especially suffered from the spiralling rise in fuel prices.

transport costs and stimulated biofuel production (see box). This coupling can have devastating implications for global poverty and food security.

The impact of climate change is a particularly difficult issue in the long-term forecasts for agricultural prices. Forecasts of the rise in temperature and its impact on agriculture over the next two decades are extremely uncertain. Climate change threatens yields in many developing countries, although most of this effect is not likely to be felt until after 2030. The World Bank assumes an overall decline in agricultural productivity of between 1–10% by 2030 (compared with a future where average global temperatures remain stable), with Canada and Europe least affected and India, Sub-Saharan Africa, and parts of Latin America most affected. Were there to be no climate change between now and 2030, global agricultural productivity would be nearly 4% higher and the world price of food 5.3% lower. Over the longer term, the impacts of climate change could be much more serious, with agricultural productivity in many developing regions, notably Africa, potentially declining much higher than the global average (Cline, 2007).

In Global Economic Prospects 2009, the World Bank has run a number of simulations to quantify possible outcomes. Should global agricultural productivity rise by only 1.2% per year on average, instead of the 2.1% projected in the baseline, then prices, rather than declining, can be expected to rise by as much as 0.3% per year. If cereal production could increase as projected without any environmental constraints, it is expected to grow by 1.5 1.5% to 2030 according to demand, and by 0.9–1.0% between 2030 and 2050 (FAO, 2006; World Bank, 2008). However, the current scenarios of losses and constraints due to climate change and environmental degradation – with no policy change – suggest that production increases could fall to 0.87% towards 2030 and only 0.5% between 2030–2050 (World Bank, 2008).

Alternatively, biofuels could have a significant impact on food prices if oil prices remain high or the cost of biofuels production declines. With a permanent increase in the rate of growth of demand for food products as source material for biofuels (as-

suming a doubling in biofuel production compared to the baseline), food prices will decline by only 0.5% a year. In general, OECD-FAO estimates confirm this sensitivity to key assumptions about yield and biofuels production (OECD-FAO, 2008).

Overall, soaring food prices are blamed for their impacts on human vulnerability. However, there are two sides to this picture. Increasing food prices do have a positive effect on net food-selling households (FAO, 2008), augmenting their incomes and allowing more possibilities for farmers to afford investments in production inputs. This underlines the need to minimize short-term price volatility and stimulate slow increases in long-term food prices, in order to enhance investments in the agricultural system and bridge the gap between developed and developing countries as well as between rural food producing and urban food consuming regions. Ideally, these developments should take the environmental aspects previously described into account to achieve sustainable agricultural systems that will meet the food demand of all the world citizens and eradicate hunger. However, increasing yield and food supply without simply continuing the conventional expansion of cropland and rangeland and use of fertilizers and pesticides – at the cost of biodiversity and future generations – will require major investments and implementation of food energy considerations in the entire food production and consumption chain.

# SEVEN OPTIONS FOR IMPROVING FOOD SECURITY

Increasing food energy efficiency provides a critical path for significant growth in food supply without compromising environmental sustainability. Seven options are proposed for the short-, mid- and long-term.

**OPTIONS WITH SHORT-TERM EFFECTS**

**1** *To decrease the risk of highly volatile prices, price regulation on commodities and larger cereal stocks should be created to buffer the tight markets of food commodities and the subsequent risks of speculation in markets.*
This includes reorganizing the food market infrastructure and institutions to regulate food prices and provide food safety nets aimed at alleviating the impacts of rising food prices and food shortage, including both direct and indirect transfers, such as a global fund to support micro-finance to boost small-scale farmer productivity.

**2** *Encourage removal of subsidies and blending ratios of first generation biofuels, which would promote a shift to higher generation biofuels based on waste (if this does not compete with animal feed), thereby avoiding the capture of cropland by biofuels.*
This includes removal of subsidies on agricultural commodities and inputs that are exacerbating the developing food crisis, and investing in shifting to sustainable food systems and food energy efficiency.

**OPTIONS WITH MID-TERM EFFECTS**

**3** *Reduce the use of cereals and food fish in animal feed and develop alternatives to animal and fish feed.*

This can be done in a "green" economy by increasing food energy efficiency using fish discards, capture and recycling of post-harvest losses and waste and development of new technology, thereby increasing food energy efficiency by 30–50% at current production levels. It also involves re-allocating fish currently used for aquaculture feed directly to human consumption, where feasible.

**4** *Support farmers in developing diversified and resilient eco-agriculture systems that provide critical ecosystem services (water supply and regulation, habitat for wild plants and animals, genetic diversity, pollination, pest control, climate regulation), as well as adequate food to meet local and consumer needs.*

This includes managing extreme rainfall and using inter-cropping to minimize dependency on external inputs like artificial fertilizers, pesticides and blue irrigation water and the development, implementation and support of green technology also for small-scale farmers.

**5** *Increased trade and improved market access can be achieved by improving infrastructure and reducing trade barriers.*

However, this does not imply a completely free market approach, as price regulation and government subsidies are crucial safety nets and investments in production. Increased market access must also incorporate a reduction of armed conflict and corruption, which has a major impact on trade and food security.

**OPTIONS WITH LONG-TERM EFFECTS**

**6** *Limit global warming, including the promotion of climate-friendly agricultural production systems and land-use policies at a scale to help mitigate climate change.*

**7** *Raise awareness of the pressures of increasing population growth and consumption patterns on sustainable ecosystem functioning.*

# CONTRIBUTORS AND REVIEWERS

**ACKNOWLEDGEMENTS**
A high number of individuals, institutions and organizations assisted in the preparation of this report at a very short notice. We are highly grateful for their inputs, assistance and advice. Thanks to the RSPB, European Bird Census Council (EBCC) and the Pan-European Common Bird Monitoring Scheme (PECBMS), which is an EBCC/BirdLife International initiative to deliver policy-relevant biodiversity indicators in Europe. Thanks also to D. Dent and Z. G. Bai, ISRIC for use of graphic material.

## LIST OF CONTRIBUTORS

Philip Bubb, UNEP-WCMC
Alison Campbell, UNEP-WCMC
Jörn Scharlemann, UNEP-WCMC
Christoph Zöckler, UNEP-WCMC
Nicola Barnard, UNEP-WCMC
Martin Jenkins, UNEP-WCMC
Valerie Kapos, UNEP-WCMC
Francine Kershaw, UNEP-WCMC
Abisha Mapendembe, UNEP-WCMC
Ieva Rucevska, UNEP GRID-Arendal
Emily Corcoran, UNEP GRID-Arendal
Kathrine Johnsen, UNEP GRID-Arendal
Åke Bjørke, UNEP GRID-Arendal
Peter Prokosch, UNEP GRID-Arendal
Ingunn Vistnes, NORUT-NIBR Finnmark
Robert Alkemade, PBL, The Netherlands
Ben ten Brink, PBL, The Netherlands
Michel Jeuken, PBL, The Netherlands
Kees Klein Goldewijk, PBL, The Netherlands
Ibrahim Thiaw, UNEP, Nairobi
Anantha Duraiappah, UNEP, Nairobi
Renate Fleiner, UNEP, Nairobi
Jacqueline Alder, UNEP, Nairobi
Yvette DieiOuadi, FAO, Rome
Mats Eriksson, ICIMOD, Nepal
Madhav Karki, ICIMOD, Nepal
Golam Rasul, ICIMOD, Nepal
Julie Dekens, ICIMOD, Nepal
Basanta Shrestha, ICIMOD, Nepal
Richard Gregory, RSPB, UK
Sara Scherr, Ecoagriculture Partners, Washington, USA
Toby Hodgkin, Bioversity International, Rome

# REFERENCES

Alcamo et al. (2003). Global estimates of water withdrawals and availability under current and future "business-as-usual" conditions. Hydrological Sciences Journal 48 (3): 339-348.

Alder et al. (2008). Forage Fish: From Ecosystems to Markets. Annual Review of Environment and Resources 33: 153-166.

Alig et al. (2004). Projecting large-scale area changes in land use and land cover for terrestrial carbon analyses. Environmental Management 33 (4): 443-456.

Alkemade et al. (2009). Framework to assess global terrestrial biodiversity: Options to reduce global biodiversity loss. Ecosystems (In press).

Anderson et al. (2004). Emerging infectious diseases of plants: pathogen pollution, climate change and agro-technological drivers. Trends in Ecology and Evolution 19 (10): 535-544.

Anderson et al. (2008). Harmful algae blooms and eutrophication: Examining linkages from selected coastal regions of the United States. Harmful Algae 8: 39-53.

Aragón-Noriega, L.E. and Calderon-Aguilera, E.A. (2000). Does damming of the Colorado River affect the nursery area of blue shrimp Litopenaeus stylirostris (Decapoda: Penaeidae) in the Upper Gulf of California? Revista de Biologia Tropical 48 (4): 867-871.

Bai, Z.G and Dent, D.L. (2006). Global Assessment of Land Degradation and Improvement: pilot study in Kenya. Report 2006/01, ISRIC - World Soil Information, Wageningen.

Bai, Z.G. and Dent, D.L. (2007). Land degradation and improvement in South Africa. 1. Identification by remote sensing. Report 2007/03, ISRIC – World Soil Information, Wageningen.

Bai et al. (2007): Land cover change and soil fertility decline in tropical regions. Turkish Journal of Agriculture and Forestry 32 (3): 195-213.

Bai et al. (2008). Global assessment of land degradation and improvement 1: identification by remote sensing. Report 2008/01, FAO/ISRIC, Rome/Wageningen.

Balmford et al. (2005). Sparing land for nature: exploring the potential impact of changes in agricultural yield on the area needed for crop production. Global Change Biology 10: 1594-1605.

Balmford et al. (2008). Global mapping of ecosystem services and conservation priorities. Proceedings of the Natural Academy of Sciences of the United States of America (PNAS) 105 (28): 9495-9500.

Banse et al. (2008). Will EU biofuel policies affect global agricultural markets? European Review of Agricultural Economics 35 (2): 117-141.

Bianchi et al. (2006). Sustainable pest regulation in agricultural landscapes: a review on landscape composition, biodiversity and natural pest control. Proceedings of the Natural Academy of Sciences of the United States of America (PNAS) 273 (1595): 1715-1727.

BirdLife (2008). Critically Endangered Birds: A Global Audit. BirdLife International, Cambridge, UK. Available online at: http://www.birdlife.org/news/news/2008/09/Complete_Critical%20Birds_superlowres.pdf [Accessed on the 20 January 2009].

Bloom, J. (2007). Food waste: out of sight, out of mind. Culinate, Portland. Available online at: (http://www.culinate.com/articles/features/wasted_food/print) [Accessed on the 20 January 2009].

Böhner, J. and Lehmkuhl, F. (2005). Environmental change modelling for Central and High Asia: Pleistocene, present and future scenarios. Boreas 32 (2): 220-231.

Brahmbhatt, M. and Christiaensen, L. (2008). Rising Food Prices in East Asia. Challenges and Policy Options. Sustainable Development Department of the East Asia and Pacific region of the World Bank, Washington D.C.

Braun, J. (2007). The World food situation. Food Policy Report 18. IFPRI, Washington D.C. Available online at: http://www.ifpri.org/pubs/fpr/pr18.pdf [Accessed on the 20 January 2009].

Bruijnzeel, L.A. (2004). Hydrological functions of tropical forests: not seeing the soil for the trees? Agriculture Ecosystems & Environment 104 (1): 185-228.

Brown, M.E. and Funk, C.C. (2008). Climate - Food security under climate change. Science 319 (5863): 580-581.

Camara, O. and Heinemaan, E. (2006). Overview of the Fertilizer Situation in Africa. African Fertilizer Summit background paper, Abuja, Nigeria, June 9–13.

CBD (2001). Status, impacts and trends of alien species that threaten ecosystems, habitats and species. CBD, Montreal. Available online at: http://www.cbd.int/doc/meetings/sbstta/sbstta-06/information/sbstta-06-inf-11-en.pdf [Accessed on the 20 January 2009].

CBD (2006). Cross-roads of Life on Earth: Exploring means to meet the 2010 Biodiversity Target. Secretariat of the Convention on Biological Diversity, Montreal, Technical Series no. 31. Available online at: http://www.mnp.nl/bibliotheek/rapporten/555050001.pdf [Accessed on the 20 January 2009].

Chapagain, A.K. and Hoekstra, A.Y. (2008). The global component of freshwater demand and supply: an assessment of virtual water flows between nations as a result of trade in agricultural and industrial products. Water International 33 (1): 19-32.

Chenje, M. and Katerere, J. (2006). Chapter 10: Invasive alien species. In: UNEP. 2006. Africa Environment Outlook 2: Our environment, our wealth. United Nations Environment Programme, Nairobi. Available online at: http://www.unep.org/DEWA/Africa/docs/en/AEO2_Our_Environ_Our_Wealth.pdf [Accessed on the 20 January 2009].

Cline, William R. (2007). Global Warming and Agriculture: Impact Estimates by Country. Center for Global Development and Peterson Institute for International Economics. Washington, D.C.

CSIRO (2008). Biosecurity and invasive species. CSIRO, Canberra, Australia. Available online: http://www.csiro.au/files/files/pl2v.pdf [Accessed on the 20 January 2009].

De Fraiture et al. (2003). Addressing the unanswered questions in global water policy: A methodology framework. Irrigation and Drainage 52 (1): 21-30.

den Biggelaar et al. (2004). The global impact of soil erosion on productivity. Advances in Agronomy 81: 1-95.

Deutsch et al. (2007). Feeding aquaculture growth through globalization: Exploitation of marine ecosystems for fishmeal. Global Environmental Change – Human and Policy Dimensions 17 (2): 238-249.

Diaz, R.J. and Rosenberg, R. (2008). Spreading dead zones and consequences for marine ecosystems. Science 321 (5891): 926-929.

Diaz et al. (2007). Biodiversity regulation of ecosystem services. In Hassan, R., Schoes, R and Ash, N. (ed.): Ecosystems and Human Well-being: Current State and Trends 1 (1): 299-329.

Earth Policy Institute (2006). Data files for Supermarkets and Service Stations Now Competing for Grain. EPI, Washington D.C. Available online at: http://www.earth-policy.org/Updates/2006/Update55_data.htm [Accessed on the 20 January 2009].

Eating ecologically. Waste. Available online at: http://www.eateco.org/Waste.htm or http://www.eateco.org/PDF/Waste.pdf [Accessed on the 20 January 2009].

EBBC (2008). European Breeding Bird Census Report. Available online at: http://www.ebcc.info/index.php?ID=367&indik%5BE_C_Fa%5D=1 [Accessed on the 20 January 2009].

EEA/SEBI 2010 (2007). Halting the loss of biodiversity by 2010: proposals for a first set of indicators to monitor progress in Europe. EEA, Copenhagen.

Eriksson et al. (2008). How does climate affect human health in the Hindu Kush-Himalaya region? Regional Health Forum 12: 11-15. Available online at: http://www.searo.who.int/LinkFiles/Regional_Health_Forum_Volume_12_No_1_How_does_climate.pdf [Accessed on the 20 January 2009].

Ethridge et al. (2006). World cotton outlook: Projections to 2015/16. Beltwide Cotton Conferences, San Antonio, Texas January 3-6, 2006. Available online at: http://www.aaec.ttu.edu/Publications/Beltwide%202006/206-234.pdf [Accessed on the 20 January 2009].

European Bird Census Council (2008). Trends of Common Birds in Europe, 2008 update. EBCC. Available online at: http://www.ebcc.info/index.php?ID=358 [Accessed on the 20 January 2009].

FAO (1998). The State of the World's Plant Genetic Resources for Food and Agriculture. FAO, Rome. Available online at: http://www.fao.org/ag/AGP/agps/PGRFA/pdf/swrshr_e.pdf [Accessed on the 20 January 2009].

FAO. 1999. Poverty and irrigated agriculture. FAO, Rome. www.fao.org

FAO (2003). World agriculture: towards 2015/2030. FAO, Rome. Available online at: ftp://ftp.fao.org/docrep/fao/004/y3557e/y3557e.pdf [Accessed on the 20 January 2009].

FAO (2004). The State of the Food Insecurity in the World 2004. FAO, Rome. Available online at: ftp://ftp.fao.org/docrep/fao/007/y5650e/y5650e00.pdf [Accessed on the 20 January 2009].

FAO (2005). The State of the Food Insecurity in the World 2005. FAO, Rome. Available online at: ftp://ftp.fao.org/docrep/fao/008/a0200e/a0200e.pdf [Accessed on the 20 January 2009].

FAO (2005b). Irrigation in Africa in Figures. Aquastat Survey—2005. FAO. Available online at: ftp://ftp.fao.org/agl/aglw/docs/wr29_eng.pdf [Accessed on the 20 January 2009].

FAO (2006). World Agriculture, towards 2030/2050. FAO, Rome. Available online at: http://www.fao.org/es/ESD/AT2050web.pdf [Accessed on the 20 January 2009].

FAO (2006b). Livestock's long shadow, pp. 416. FAO, Rome. Available online at: ftp://ftp.fao.org/docrep/fao/010/a0701e/a0701e.pdf [Accessed on the 20 January 2009].

FAO (2008): The state of food and agriculture 2008. FAO, Rome. Available online at: http://www.fao.org/docrep/011/i0100e/i0100e00.htm [Accessed on the 20 January 2009].

FAO (2008b). Climate Change and Desert Locusts. FAO, Rome. Available online at: http://www.fao.org/ag/locusts/en/activ/1307/climate/index.html [Accessed on the 20 January 2009].

FAOSTAT (2009). FAOSTAT. Available online at: http://faostat.fao.org/default.aspx [Accessed on the 20 January 2009].

FAPRI (2008). U.S. and World Agricultural Outlook. FAPRI, Iowa. Available online at: http://www.fapri.iastate.edu/outlook2008/text/OutlookPub2008.pdf [Accessed on the 20 January 2009].

Fargione et al. (2008). Land clearing and the biofuel carbon debt. Science 319 (5867): 1235-1238.

Farrell, G. and Schulten, G. G. M. (2002). Larger Grain Borer in Africa, A History of Efforts to Limit its Impact. Integrated Pest Management Reviews 7 (2): 67–84.

Fischlin et al. (2007): Ecosystems, their properties, goods, and services. Climate Change 2007: Impacts, Adaptation and Vulnerability. Contribution of Working Group II to the Fourth Assessment Report of the Intergovernmental Panel on Climate Change, M.L. Parry, O.F. Canziani, J.P. Palutikof, P.J. van der Linden and C.E. Hanson, (ed.), Cambridge University Press, Cambridge.

Faurès et al. (2000). The FAO irrigated area forecast for 2030. FAO, Rome.

Fitzherbert et al. (2008). How will oil palm expansion affect biodiversity? Trends in Ecology and Evolution 23 (10): 528-545.

Foley et al. (2005). Global Consequences of Land Use. Science 309: 570-575.

Gan, J. (2004). Risk and damage of southern pine beetle outbreaks under global climate change. Forest Ecology and Management 191 (1-3): 61-71.

Gaston et al. (2003). Rates of species introduction to a remote oceanic island. Proceedings of the Royal Society of London Series B-Biological Sciences 270 (1519): 1091-1098.

Gerten et al. (2008). Causes of change in 20th century global river discharge. Geophysical research letters 35, L20405, doi:10.1029/2008GL035258.

GISP (Global Invasive Species Programme) (2008). Invasive Alien Species – A Growing Global Threat. Available online at: http://www.gisp.org/ecology/IAS.asp [Accessed on the 20 January 2009].

GISP (Global Invasive Species Programme). (2006). Invasive Species and Poverty: Exploring the Links. Available online at: http://www.gisp.org/publications/Brochures/invasivesandpoverty.pdf [Accessed on the 20 January 2009].

GRAIN (2008). Seized: The 2008 land grab for food and financial security. GRAIN briefing, October 2008.

Green et al. (2005). Sparing land for nature: exploring the potential impact of changes in agricultural yield on the area needed for crop production. Global Change Biology 10 (11): 1594-1605.

Groombridge, B. and Jenkins, M.D. (2002). World atlas of biodiversity: earth's living resources in the 21st century. University of California Press, California, USA.

Hanasaki et al. (2008a). An integrated model for the assessment of global water resources Part 1: Model description and input meteorological forcing. Hydrology and Earth System Sciences 12 (4): 1007-1025.

Hanasaki et al. (2008b). An integrated model for the assessment of global water resources Part 2: Applications and assessments. Hydrology and Earth System Sciences 12 (4): 1027-1037.

Henao, J. and Baanante, C. (2006). Agricultural Production and Soil Nutrient Mining in Africa. Summary of IFDC Technical Bulletin. IFDC, Alabama, USA.

Henningsson et al. (2004). The value of resource efficiency in the food industry: a waste minimization project in East Anglia, UK. Journal of Cleaner Production 12 (5): 505-512.

HYDE, History Database of the Global Environment, v 3.0, http://www.mnp.nl/hyde.

IAASTD (2008). International Assessment of Agricultural Knowledge, Science and Technology for Development. IAASTD, Washington, D.C. Available online at: http://www.agassessment.org/docs/IAASTD_GLOBAL_SDM_JAN_2008.pdf [Accessed on the 20 January 2009)

ICIMOD (2008). Food Security in the Hindu Kush-Himalayan Region. ICIMOD, Chengdu.

IFPRI (2006). Annual report 2005-2006. IFPRI, Washington, D.C. Available online at: http://www.ifpri.org/pubs/books/ar2005/ar05.pdf [Accessed on the 20 January 2009].

IFPRI (2007). The World Food Situation: New Driving Forces and Required Actions. IFPRI, Washington D.C. Available online at: http://www.ifpri.org/pubs/fpr/pr18.pdf [Accessed on the 20 January 2009].

IFPRI (2008). The Challenge of Hunger in 2008, Global Hunger Index, IFPRI, Washington D.C. Available online at: http://www.ifpri.org/pubs/cp/ghio8.asp#dl [Accessed on the 20 January 2009].

International Fertilizer Association (2008). IFADATA. Available online at: http://www.fertilizer.org/ifa/ifadata/search [Accessed on the 20 January 2009].

International Monetary Fund (IMF) (2008). IMF Primary Commodity Prices, monthly data (CSV file) for 8 price indices and 49 actual price series, 1980 - current. IMF, Washington D.C. Available online at: http://www.imf.org/external/np/res/commod/index.asp [Accessed on the 20 January 2009].

IPPC (2004). RIO/Uppsala Armed COnflict Dataset. International Peace Research Institute, Oslo (PRIO), Department of Peace and Conflict Research, Uppsala University, Stockholm International Peace Research Institute 2003.

IPCC (2007). Climate Change 2007: Impacts, Adaptation and Vulnerability. Contribution of Working Group II to the Fourth Assessment Report of the Intergovernmental Panel on Climate Change. M.L. Parry, O.F. Canziani, J.P. Palutikof, P.J. van der Linden and C.E. Hanson (ed.). Cambridge University Press, Cambridge, UK.

IUCN (2008). Red list of threatened species. IUCN, Gland, Switzerland. Available online at: http://www.iucnredlist.org/ [Accessed on the 20 January 2009].

Jianchu, X., A. Shrestha, et al. (2007). The Melting Himalayas: Regional challenges and local impacts of climate change on mountain ecosystems and livelihoods. ICIMOD Technical Paper. Katmandu, Nepal, ICIMOD.

Kader, A. A. (2005). Increasing food availability by reducing postharvest losses of fresh produce. Proceedings of the 5th International Postharvest Symposium, Mencarelli, F. (Eds.) and Tonutti P. Acta Horticulturae, ISHS.

Kantor et al. (1999). Estimating and addressing America's food losses. American Journal of Agricultural Economics 81 (5): 1325-1325

Kenis et al. (2009). Ecological effects of invasive alien insects. Biological Invasions 11 (1): 21-45.

Keyzer et al. (2005). Diet shifts towards meat and the effects on cereal use: can we feed the animals in 2030? Ecological Economics 55 (2): 187-202.

Klein, Goldewijk K. (2001). Estimating global land use change over the past 300 years: the HYDE database. Global Biogeochemical Cycles 15 (2): 417-433.

Klein, Goldewijk K. (2005). Three centuries of global population growth: A spatial referenced population density database for 1700 – 2000. Population and Environment, 26 (4): 343-367.

Klein, Goldewijk K. and Beusen, A. (2009). Long term dynamic modeling of global population and built-up area in a spatially explicit way. In preparation.

Knight, A. and Davis, C. (2007). What a waste! Surplus fresh foods research project, S.C.R.A.T.C.H. Available online at: http://www.veoliatrust.org/docs/Surplus_Food_Research.pdf [Accessed on the 20 January 2009].

Kremen, C. and Chaplin-Kramer, R. (2007). Insects as providers of ecosystem services: crop pollination and pest control. In Insect Conservation Biology: proceedings of the Royal Entomological Society's 23rd Symposium. A.J.A. Stewart, T.R. New and O.T. Lewis (ed.). CABI Publishing, Wallingford.

Lal, R. (1998). Soil erosion impact on agronomic productivity and environment quality. Critical reviews in plant sciences 17: 319-464

Le Maitre et al. (2004). Alien plant invasions in South Africa: driving forces and the human dimension. South African Journal of Science 100 (1), 103–112.

Liu, X.D. and Chen, B.D. (2000). Climatic warming in the Tibetan Plateau during recent decades. International Journal of Climatology 20 (14): 1729-1742.

Lobell et al. (2008). Prioritizing climate change adaptation needs for food security in 2030. Science 319 (5863): 607-610.

Long et al. (2006). Food for thought: Lower-than-expected crop yield stimulation with rising $CO_2$ concentrations. Science 312 (5782): 1918-1921.

Lundqvist et al. (2008). Saving Water: From Field to Fork – Curbing Losses and Wastage in the Food Chain. SIWI Policy Brief. SIWI. Available online at: http://www.siwi.org/documents/Resources/Policy_Briefs/PB_From_Filed_to_fork_2008.pdf [Accessed on the 20 January 2009].

MA (2005). Ecosystems & Human Well-being: Wetlands & Water. World Resources Institute, Washington, DC.

Macdonald, I. A. W. (1994). Global change and alien invasion, implications for biodiversity and protected area management. In: Biodiversity and global change. O. T. Solbrig, P. G. van Emden and W. J. van Oordt (ed.). Wallingford-Oxon, UK. CAB International.

Mack et al. (2000). Biotic Invasions: causes epidemiology, global consequences and control. Ecological Applications 10 (3): 689-710.

Maizel et al. (1998). Historical interrelationships between population settlement and farmland in the conterminous United States, 1790 to 1990. In: T.D. Sisk (ed.) Perspectives on the land use history of North America: a context for understanding our changing environment, U.S. Geological Survey, Biological Resources Division, Biological Science Report, USGS/BRD/BSR 1998-0003.

Malcolm et al. (2002). Estimated migration rates under scenarios of global climate change. Journal of Biogeography 29 (7): 835-849.

Meehl et al. (2007). Global Climate Projections. In: Climate Change 2007: The Physical Science Basis. Contribution of Working Group I to the Fourth Assessment Report of the Intergovernmental Panel on Climate Change. Solomon. S., D. Qin, M. Manning, Z. Chen, M. Marquis, K.B. Averyt, M. Tignor and H.L. Miller (ed.). Cambridge University Press, Cambridge, United Kingdom and New York, N.Y.

Millennium Ecosystem Assessment (2005). Ecosystems and Human Well-being: Biodiversity Synthesis. World Resources Institute, Washington. D.C.

Mitchell et al. (2005). Sediments, nutrients and pesticide residues in event flow conditions in streams of the Mackay Whitsunday Region, Australia. Marine Pollution Bulletin 51 (1-4): 23-36.

Mongabay, (2008). Available online at: http://news.mongabay.com/2008/1119-madagascar.html [Accessed on the 20 January 2009].

Mooney, H.A. and Hobbs, R.J. (ed.) (2000). Invasive Species in a Changing World. Island Press. Washington, D.C..

NEPAD (2003). Action Plan for the Environment Initiative. New Partnership for Africa's Development (NEPAD), Midland. Available online at: http://www.nepad.org/2005/files/documents/113.pdf [Accessed on the 20 January 2009].

Nepstad et al. (2007). Mortality of large trees and lianas following experimental drought in an amazon forest. Ecology 88 (9): 2259-2269.

OECD (2008). Rising Food Prices, Causes and Consequences. OECD, Paris. Available online at: http://www.oecd.org/dataoecd/54/42/40847088.pdf [Accessed on the 20 January 2009].

OECD-FAO (2008). Agricultural Outlook 2008-2017. OECD, Paris. Available online at: http://www.agri-outlook.org/dataoecd/44/18/40713249.pdf [Accessed on the 20 January 2009].

Oerke et al. (1994). Crop Production and Crop Protection: Estimated losses in major food and cash crops. Elsevier Science B.V, Amsterdam.

OTA (1993). Harmful non-indigenous species in the United States. Office of Technology Assessment, United States Congress, Washington D.C.

Parry et al. (2005). Climate change, global food supply and risk of hunger. Philosophical Transactions of the Royal Society of London B-Biological Sciences 360 (1463): 2125-2138.

Pimentel et al. (2001). Economic and environmental threats of alien plant, animal and microbe invasions. Agriculture, Ecosystems and Environment 84 (1): 1-20.

Pimentel, D. (ed.) (2002). Biological Invasions: Economic and Environmental Costs of Alien Plant, Animal, and Microbe Species. CRC Press, Boca Raton, Florida.

Pimentel et al. (2005). Update on the environmental and economic costs associated with alien-invasive species in the United States. Ecological Economics 52 (3): 273-288.

Pingali, P. (2004). Westernization of Asian Diets and the transformation of food systems: Implications for research and policy. ESA Working Paper No. 04-17. FAO, Rome.

Pingali, P. and Khwaja, Y. (2004) Globalization of Indian diets and the transformation of food supply systems. Inaugural Keynote Address on 17th Annual Conference of the Indian Society of Agricultural Marketing, Hyderabad, 5-7 February, 2004.

Pingali, P. and Rosegrant, M.W. (1998). Supplying Wheat for Asia's Increasingly Westernized Diets. American Journal of Agricultural 80 (5): 954-959.

Pinstrup-Andersen, P. and Pandya-Lorch, R. (1998). Food security and sustainable use of natural resources: A 2020 Vision. Ecological Economics 26 (1): 1-10.

Potere, D. and Schneider, A. (2007). A critical look at representations of urban areas in global maps. Geojournal 69 (1-2): 55-80.

Pyke et al. (2008). Current practices and future opportunities for policy on climate change and invasive species. Conservation Biology 22 (3): 585-592.

Rabalais, N.N., Turner, R.E. and Wiseman, W.J. (1999). Hypoxia in the northern Gulf of Mexico: Linkages with the Mississippi River, p 297-322 in: Kumpf, H., Steidinger, K. and Sherman, K. (eds), The Gulf of Mexico Large Marine Ecosystem – Assessment, Sustainability and Management. Blackwell Science, U.S.

Rangi, D.K. (2004). Invasive alien species: agriculture and development, Proceedings of a global synthesis workshop on biodiversity loss and species extinctions: managing risk in a changing world location. UNEP, Nairobi.

Reardon et al. (2003). The rise of supermarkets in Africa, Asia, and Latin America. American Journal of Agricultural Economics 85 (5): 1140-1146.

Rees, G. and Collins, D. N. (2004). Final Technical Report, Volume 2: An assessment of the impacts of deglaciation on the water resources of the Himalaya. DFID KAR Project No. R7980.

Rockstrom, J. and Barron, J. (2007). Water productivity in rainfed systems: overview of challenges and analysis of opportunities in water scarcity prone savannahs. Irrigation sceince 25: 299-311.

Rockstrom et al. (2007a). Assessing the water challenge of a new green revolution in developing countries. Proceedings of the Natural Academy of Sciences of the United States of America (PNAS) 104 (5): 6253-6260.

Rockstrom et al. (2007b). Rainwater harvesting to enhance water productivity of rainfed agriculture in the semi-arid Zimbabwe. Physics and Chemistry of the World 32 (15-18): 1068-1073.

Rosegrant, M.W. and Cai, X.M. (2002). Global water demand and supply projections part - 2. Results and prospects to 2025. Water International 27 (2): 170-182.

Rossman, A. (2009). The impact of invasive fungi on agricultural ecosystems in the United States. Biological Invasions 11 (1): 97-107.

Rost et al. (2008). Agricultural green and blue water consumption and its influence on the global water system. Water Resources Research 44 (9).

Sala et al. (2000). Global biodiversity scenarios for the year 2100. Science 287 (5459): 1770-1774.

Sanchez, Pedro A. (2002). Soil Fertility and Hunger in Africa. Science 205 (5562): 2019-2020.

Schmidhuber, J. and Tubiello, F.N. (2007). Global food security under climate change. Proceedings of the Natural Academy of Sciences of the United States of America (PNAS) 104 (50): 19703–19708.

Searchinger et al. (2008). Use of US croplands for biofuels increases greenhouse gases through emissions from land-use change. Science 319 (5867): 1238-1240.

Sebastian, K. (2007). GIS/Spatial Analysis Contribution to 2008 WDR: Technical Notes on Data & Methodologies. Back-ground paper for the WDR 2008. Available online at: http://siteresources.worldbank.org/IN-TWDR2008/Resources/2795087-1191427986785/SebastianK_ch2_GIS_input_report.pdf [Accessed on the 20 January 2009].

Seitzinger, S. and Lee, R. (2008). Land-based sources of nutrients to Large Marine Ecosystems. P. 81- 97, in Sherman, K. and Hempel, G. (Eds). The UNEP Large Marine Ecosystem Report: A perspective on changing conditions in LMEs of the world's Regional Seas. UNEP Regional Seas Report and Studies No. 182. United Nations Environment Programme. Nairobi, Kenya.

Shen et al. (2008). Projection of future world water withdrawals under SRES scenarios: Water withdrawal. Hydrological sciences journal 53 (1): 11-33.

Sherman, K. and Hempel, G. (2008). Perspectives on Regional Seas and the Large Marine Ecosystem Approach. P. 3- 21 in Sherman, K. and Hempel, G. (Eds), The UNEP Large Marine Ecosystem Report: A perspective on changing conditions in LMEs of the world's Regional Seas. UNEP Regional Seas Report and Studies No. 182. United Nations Environment Programme. Nairobi, Kenya.

Shrestha et al. (1999). Maximum temperature trends in the Himalaya and its vicinity: An analysis based on temperature records from Nepal for the period 1971-94. Journal of Climate 12 (9): 2775-2786.

Slater et al. (2007). Climate change, agricultural policy and poverty reduction – how much do we know? Natural Resource Perspectives 109: 1-6.

Smakhtin et al. (2004). Taking into account environmental requirements in global scale water resources assessments. Comprehensive assessment of water resources management in agriculture. Research report 2. International Water Management Institute, Colombo.

Smil, V. (2000). Feeding the World: A Challenge for the Twenty-First Century. MIT Press, Cambridge, MA, USA.

Song et al. (2008). Different responses of invasive and native species to elevated $CO_2$ concentration. Acta Oecolo 35 (1): 128-135.

Stehfest et al. (2008). Climate benefits of changing diet, Climatic Change, in press.

Stern Review (2006). The Economics of Climate Change, Part II: The Impacts of Climate Change on Growth and Development, pp. 67 – 73. Stern Review, UK.

Stern Review (2008). International assessment of agricultural science and technology. Available online at: http://maps.grida.no/go/graphic/go/collection/iaastd-international-assessment-of-agricultural-science-and-technology-for-development [Accessed on the 20 January 2009].

Stockholm Environment Institute (2005). Sustainable Pathways to Attain the Millennium Development Goals - Assessing the Key Role of Water, Energy and Sanitation. Available online at: http://www.sei.se/SustM-DG31Auglowres.pdf [Accessed on the 20 January 2009].

Stocking, M. (1986). The cost of soil erosion in Zimbabwe in terms of the loss of three major nutrients. Consultant's Working Paper No. 3., Soil Conservation Programme. Rome, FAO Land and Water Division.

Stoorvogel et al. (1993a). Calculating Soil Nutrient Balances in Africa at Different Scales 1. Supra-national Scale. Fertilizer Research 35 (3): 227-235.

Tilman et al. (2002). Agricultural sustainability and intensive production practices. Science 418 (6898): 671-677.

TSBF-CIAT (2006). Integrated Soil Fertility Management in the Tropics. CIAT, Cali, Colombia.

Tscharntke et al. (2007). Conservation biological control and enemy diversity on a landscape scale. Biological Control 43 (3): 294-309.

Tubiello, F.N. and Fischer, G. (2006). Reducing climate change impacts on agriculture: Global and regional effects of mitigation, 2000–2080. Technological Forecasting and Social Change 74 (7): 1030-1056.

Turner, R. E. and Rabalais, N. N. (1991). Changes in Mississippi River water quality this century. Implications for coastal food webs. BioScience (41): 140-148.

UN (2007). World Urbanization Prospects 2007. UN, New York. Available online at: http://www.un.org/esa/population/publications/wup2007/2007WUP_ExecSum_web.pdf [Accessed on the 20 January 2009].

UN Population Division (2007). UN 2006 population revision. UN, New York. Available online at: http://esa.un.org/unpp/ [Accessed on the 20 January 2009].

UN (2008). United Nations, Department of Economic and Social Affairs, Population Division.

UNCTAD (2006). Trade and Environment Review 2006. UNACTAD, Geneva, Switzerland. Available online at: http://www.unctad.org/en/docs/ditcted200512_en.pdf [Accessed on the 20 January 2009].

UNCTAD (2007). The Least Developed Countries Report 2007. UNACTAD, Geneva, Switzerland. Available online at: http://www.unctad.org/en/docs/ldc2007_en.pdf [Accessed on the 20 January 2009].

UNDP (1996). United Nations Development Programme, Human Development Report 1996. UNDP, New York. Available online at: http://hdr.undp.org/en/reports/global/hdr1996/papers/ [Accessed on the 20 January 2009].

UNDP (2008). Annual Report 2008. UNDP, New York. Available online at: http://www.undp.org/publications/annualreport2008/pdf/IAR2008_ENG_low.pdf [Accessed on the 20 January 2009].

UNEP (1994). Land Degradation in South Asia: Its Severity, Causes and Effects upon the People. INDP/UNEP/FAO. World Soil Resources Report 78.

UNEP (2001). GLOBIO. Global methodology for mapping human impacts on the biosphere. UNEP/DEWA/TR.01-3. Available online at: http://www.globio.info/download.cfm?File=region/polar/globioreporthires.pdf [Accessed on the 20 January 2009].

UNEP (2004). The GEO-3 Scenarios 2002-2032 Quantification and Analysis of Environmental Impacts. UNEP/RIVM Bilthoven, Netherlands. Available online at: http://www.rivm.nl/bibliotheek/rapporten/402001022.html [Accessed on the 20 January 2009].

UNEP (2005). Fall of the Water. UNEP/GRID-Arendal, Arendal, Norway. Available online at: http://www.grida.no/_documents/himalreport_scr.pdf [Accessed on the 20 January 2009].

UNEP (2007). Global Outlook for Snow and Ice. UNEP, Nairobi. Available online at: http://www.unep.org/geo/geo_ice/PDF/full_report_LowRes.pdf [Accessed on the 20 January 2009].

UNEP (2007) . The Global Environment Outlook Report. UNEP, Nairobi. Available online at: http://www.unep.org/geo/geo4/report/GEO-4_Report_Full_en.pdf [Accessed on the 20 January 2009].

UNEP (2008). In Dead Water. Merging of Climate Change With Pollution, Over-Harvest, and Infestations in the World's Fishing Grounds. UNEP/GRID-Arendal, Arendal, Norway. Available online at: http://www.grida.no/_res/site/file/publications/InDeadWater_LR.pdf [Accessed on the 20 January 2009].

UNICEF (2005). Niger Crisis Appeal. Niger, May 2005. UNICEF, Niger. Available online at: http://www.unicef.org/emerg/files/NigerCrisisAppeal-24May2005.pdf [Accessed on the 20 January 2009].

USBC (2001). Statistical abstract of the United States, US bureau of the Census, US Government printing office, Washington D.C.

van Wilgen et al. (2007). A biome-scale assessment of the impact of invasive alien plants on ecosystem services in South Africa. Journal of Environmental Management 89 (4): 336-349.

van Wuijckhuise et al. (2006): Bluetongue in the Netherlands; description of the first clinical cases and differential diagnosis; Common symptoms just a little different and in too many herds. Tijdschr. Diergeneesk 131 (18): 649-654.

Vidal, J. (2005). More than 30% of our food is thrown away – and its costing billions a year. The Guardian, Guardian Media and News, UK. Available online at: http://guardian.co.uk/print/0,,5171494-103690,00.html [Accessed on the 20 January 2009].

Vilà et al. (2006) Linking plant invasions to environmental change. In: Canadell J., Pataki D. and Pitelka L. (ed.) Terrestrial Ecosystems in a Changing World pp. 115-124. Springer, Berlin.

Voices Newsletter. 2006. Increasing post-harvest success for smallholder farmers. No: 79: Available online at: http://www.farmradio.org/english/partners/voices/Voices_79.pdf [Accessed on the 20 January 2009].

Ward et al. (1999). Gray leaf spot: a disease of global importance in maize production. Plant disease 83 (10): 884-895.

WHO (2007). The World Health Report. A Safer Future. Global Public Health Security in the 21st Century. WHO, Geneva, Switzerland. Available at: http://www.who.int/whr/2007/whr07_en.pdf [Accessed on the 20 January 2009].

Winiger et al. (2005). Karakorum-Hindukush-western Himalaya: assessing high-altitude water resources. Hydrological Processes 19 (12): 23-29-2338.

Wodon et al. (2008). Poverty impact of higher food prices in Sub-Saharan Africa and policy responses. Mimeo, World Bank, Washington D.C.

Wood et al. (2000). Pilot Analysis of Global Ecosystems: Agro-ecosystems. A Joint Study by International Food Policy Research Institute and World Resources Institute, Washington, D.C.

World Bank (2007). World Development Report 2007: Development and the Next Generation. World Bank, Washington, D.C.

World Bank (2008). Rising Food and Fuel Prices: Addressing the Risks to Future Generations. World Bank, Washington, D.C. Available online at: http://siteresources.worldbank.org/DEVCOMMEXT/Resources/Food-Fuel.pdf?resourceurlname=Food-Fuel.pdf [Accessed on the 20 January 2009].

World Bank (Double Jeopardy: Responding to High Food and Fuel Prices. World Bank, Washington, D.C. Available online at: http://siteresources.worldbank.org/NEWS/MiscContent/21828409/G8-HL-summit-paper.pdf [Accessed on the 20 January 2009].

World Bank (2009). Global Economic Prospects: Commodities at the Crossroads. World Bank, Washington, D.C. Available online at: http://siteresources.worldbank.org/INTGEP2009/Resources/10363_WebPDF-w47.pdf [Accessed on the 20 January 2009].

World Urbanization Prospects: The 2007 Revision. CD-ROM Edition - Data in digital form (POP/ DB/WUP/Rev.2007)

WRAP (2008). Food waste report 2: The food we waste. WRAP, U.K. Available online at: http://www.wrap.org.uk/downloads/The_Food_We_Waste_v2__2_.d3471041.5635.pdf [Accessed on the 20 January 2009].

WRI (2003). Watersheds of Asia and Oceania. WRI, Washington D.C. Available online at: http://earthtrends.wri.org/maps_spatial/watersheds/asiaocea.php [Accessed on the 20 January 2009].

Yang et al. (2003). A water resources threshold and its implications for food security. Environmental science and technology 37 (14): 3048-3054.

Zhang et al. (2007). Detection of Bemisia tabaci remains in predator guts using a sequence-characterized amplified region marker. Entomologica experimentalis et applicata 123 (1): 81-90.

Zhu et al. (2000). Genetic diversity and disease control in rice. Nature 406: 718-722